PERGAMON INTERNATIONAL LIBRARY
of Science, Technology, Engineering and Social Studies
*The 1000-volume original paperback library in aid of education,
industrial training and the enjoyment of leisure*
Publisher: Robert Maxwell, M.C.

The Manager
and the Environment

D1621079

4

THE PERGAMON TEXTBOOK
INSPECTION COPY SERVICE

An inspection copy of any book published in the Pergamon International Library will
gladly be sent to academic staff without obligation for their consideration for course adoption
or recommendation. Copies may be retained for a period of 60 days from receipt and
returned if not suitable. When a particular title is adopted or recommended for adoption
for class use and the recommendation results in a sale of 12 or more copies, the inspection
copy may be retained with our compliments. The Publishers will be pleased to receive
suggestions for revised edition and new titles to be published in this important International
Library.

ENVIRONMENTAL SCIENCES AND APPLICATIONS

Series Editors: Asit K. Biswas
Margaret R. Biswas

Titles in the series

NOTICE TO READERS

The Manager
and the Environment

GENERAL THEORY AND PRACTICE OF
ENVIRONMENTAL MANAGEMENT

by

JACK G. BEALE

PERGAMON PRESS
OXFORD · NEW YORK · TORONTO · SYDNEY · PARIS · FRANKFURT

U.K.	Pergamon Press Ltd., Headington Hill Hall, Oxford OX3 0BW, England
U.S.A.	Pergamon Press Inc., Maxwell House, Fairview Park, Elmsford, New York 10523, U.S.A.
CANADA	Pergamon of Canada Ltd., Suite 104, 150 Consumers Road, Willowdale, Ontario, Canada M2J 1P9
AUSTRALIA	Pergamon Press (Aust.) Pty. Ltd., P.O. Box 544, Potts Point, N.S.W. 2011, Australia
FRANCE	Pergamon Press SARL, 24 rue des Ecoles, 75240 Paris, Cedex 05, France
FEDERAL REPUBLIC OF GERMANY	Pergamon Press GmbH, 6242 Kronberg-Taunus, Pferdstrasse 1, Federal Republic of Germany

First edition 1980

British Library Cataloguing in Publication Data

Beale, Jack G
The manager and the environment.
1. Environmental protection
I. Title
301.31   TD170   79-40712
ISBN 0-08-024043-7 (Hard cover)
ISBN 0-08-024044-5 (Flexicover)

Printed in Great Britain by Biddles Ltd, Guildford, Surrey

Contents

Contents

List of Illustrations

Foreword

During the past decade the world has seen the beginning of one of the quietest and most profound revolutions in the history of human society. It has its roots in the emergence of environment as a major public issue.

Concern for the environment first emerged as an important public issue during the 1960s. At that time it was perceived almost exclusively as a concern of the industrialized countries, rooted in the growing evidences that the processes of urbanization and industrialization which had produced such benefits for these societies were also producing unexpected costs in the pollution of air and water, destruction of natural resources and deterioration in the quality of urban life. This was the general perception when the United Nations took the decision to hold a conference on the human environment in Stockholm in June 1972 which moved the environment issue into the centre of the world's political arena and established it as an important item on the agenda of governments throughout the world.

Developing countries reacted first with a mixture of indifference, suspicion and hostility at what many regarded as the latest "fad of the rich" which threatened to divert attention and resources from the primary needs of the developing countries for whom underdevelopment and poverty constituted the most acute and immediate threat to the environment of their peoples. At the insistence of the developing countries the agenda of the Stockholm conference and the concept of environment were broadened to include issues of more direct and immediate concern to them, including loss of productive soil and the march of the deserts, the management of tropical ecosystems, provision of pure water for human use, and the problems of human settlements. They also forced a clear recognition of the relationship between environment and development, of the truth that it is through the process of development that the environment is affected, either positively or negatively, and that it is through the planning and management of the development process that we must deal with the care and protection of the environment.

This broadened approach to the environment issue and the relationship between environment and development became the basis for developing country participation in the Stockholm conference and the rapid evolution of their interest in environment. It also had a decisive effect on shaping the recommendations of the conference and the subsequent content and direction of the United Nations Environment Programme. It gave rise to the concept of "eco-development" based on harmonizing the economic, ecological and social factors so as to make best use of indigenous resources and skills in producing a sustainable pattern of development that will best accord with the values, needs and aspirations of the people concerned.

But it was not enough simply to articulate this new approach to development. UNEP realized early in its life as an agency that agreed international philosophy would have to be backed by practical assistance to member states at every level of activity. At the Second Governing Council meeting of UNEP in 1974 it was resolved to give emphasis to institution-building at the national level. The almost immediate response to this resolve was a call on UNEP to provide advice to many of its member states. Experienced advisers were few at that time and even fewer were the blueprints or precedents for successful going operations.

This book has to some extent originated out of some of the first of UNEP's advisory missions to developing nations (the first Beale mission was to Thailand in November 1974). The author's views of course are his own, reflecting also his personal experience as practising political head of an environment Ministry, one of the first anywhere in the world. (Jack Beale led the move which eventually resulted in the establishment of comprehensive environmental control systems for the whole Australian continent.) His subsequent experience is translated into "real-life" international situations. I count myself fortunate to have met him at his post in Australia early (in March 1971) when I was organizing UNCHE, and to have had my own conviction that environmental programmes could be made to work reinforced at that early stage of my own involvement in environmental administration. Having urged Jack Beale to continue his international work after retirement from politics late in 1973, I welcome this book as a notable example of the kind of dynamic and creative leadership he continues to bring to the world environmental movement.

As he points out, a good theory does not necessarily get anything done practically. Practice is in the hands of the skilled manager, administrator, and legislative draftsman. If these people are only given slogans and abstract philosophies to translate into purposeful action, and this is usual, only rhetoric will result. If, on the other hand, they have a clear idea of the kinds of institutions they need to build, the linkages they need to forge between new and existing institutions, the techniques and tools available to them, and the means by which they should be delivering the environmental goods to people, these same managers and administrators will be able to achieve the results their leaders call for.

To date, there has been far too little recognition of the need for a new generation of governmental mechanisms to deliver environmental programmes. Jack Beale has set out what amounts to a general theory and practice of environmental management and administration. He brings to bear on this subject his broad academic, administrative and political knowledge allied with practical experience in some sixty countries in all continents. This, plus his proven ability to get things done in many diverse fields, makes him one of few fully equipped to give a lead to managers, planners and administrators in this relatively new field.

I commend this book to all those at every level of management who by "Making Things Happen" affect the quality of the environment. Not only does it provide for managers a wealth of practical insights and information which will be invaluable in helping them to make environmentally sound decisions, but it also demonstrates in clear and compelling fashion the crucial responsibility which managers have for the preservation of the environment on which human survival depends.

Maurice F. Strong

First Executive Director
United Nations Environment Programme (UNEP).

Chairman, Executive Board
The International Union for Conservation
of Nature and Natural Resources (IUCN).

Prologue

"An anecdote to introduce a book?" I thought about it. Then I remembered a scene of many years ago. Excitement and concern pervaded the crowded room. Students were enrolling in first year engineering studies. Some were perturbed by rumours about the intricacies of a mysterious mathematical subject called calculus.

Later, searching for text books, the title *Calculus Made Easy* stood out. "That's for me," I thought. On the first page was the comforting old Simian proverb: *"What one fool can do, another can."*

I read on. Quickly my concern evaporated. Avidly I devoured the contents and easily cleared the first calculus hurdle. True, there were to be other hurdles. But from this simple practical introduction I gradually developed sufficient competence in this unfamiliar field of mathematics to be able to use it effectively in professional engineering. I never forgot my calculus text and the little adage on the first page.

A complex environmental policy administration field also arouses concern—even antagonism—in beginners, young and old "fools" alike. This book is designed to help readers to achieve competence in emerging systems of *environmental management.*

Apart from other difficulties, novice environmental administrators face a bewildering jargon—*ecosystem, biosphere, biological desert, eco-development.* There is no need to be intimidated. As with calculus, the jargon can be taken easily if its context is understood. Environmentalists are merely talking about particular aspects of the relationship between mankind and his works, and nature. Which isn't something new—Man has had aeons of experience with his earthy surroundings.

Planners and administrators in all systems of government are deluged with a baffling array of advice on environmental problems. Often the input from experts is conflicting. Worldwide, diverse forms of government and differing cultures make it harder to use set solutions. Decision makers usually display their bewilderment through inadvertent, piecemeal, short-sighted and indecisive actions which can only exacerbate the environmental problem they set out originally to solve.

Nevertheless many managers have been able to achieve economic and social advances and at the same time afford effective protection to the environment. An objective of this book is to alert those responsible to opportunities for policy, legislative, administrative and technical initiatives which alone can provide a basis for sound environmental action.

So read on. Advance your competence in environmental management to help make your full contribution to the attainment of improved local, regional and global environments. Others have been successful in *making things happen*. Bear in mind the old Simian proverb.

Jack G. Beale

Sydney, Australia
1978.

Acknowledgements

During the preparation of this book help was given by numerous people from many walks of life. They are representative of a wide variety of governmental agencies, universities, research organizations, professions, industries, business and special interest groups. Discussions with them spread over some sixty countries covering all continents. I am grateful to them for sharing knowledge and experience, thereby contributing to this book.

Its genesis as a publication owes something to discussions some years ago with Maurice F. Strong, the first Executive Director of the United Nations Environment Programme (UNEP), who encouraged me to extend my international environmental activities, including consultancies with UNEP. He was convinced that upgrading of environmental practice was as important as promoting theory. Mr. Strong and his successor, Dr. Mostafa K. Tolba, prompted me to set down some thoughts on ways to achieve practical national environmental initiatives.

Thanks are due to those who gave their time to orient my thoughts in the preparation stages and offer comment based on their own particular expertise and experience. Prominent among these are: Mr. C. Suriyakumaran, Regional Representative for Asia and the Pacific; Mr. John H. Robertson, Senior Programme Officer, and Dr. Adriano Buzzati-Traverso, Senior Scientific Adviser, of UNEP; Prof. Robert H. Twiss, College of Environmental Design, University of California at Berkeley; Mr. M. E. D. Poore, The International Union for Conservation of Nature and Natural Resources (IUCN), Switzerland; Dr. Asit Biswas, Senior Consultant to the UN System and OECD, and Mrs. Margaret R. Biswas; Dr. Peter J. Reynolds,

Department of Environment, Canada; Prof. Jerzy Kozlowski and Dr. Magdalena Janota, Instytut Ksztaltowania Srodowiska (Institute for Environmental Development), Poland; Dr. William H. Matthews, Senior Research Scholar, International Institute for Applied Systems Analysis (IIASA), Austria; Dr. Manuel Arroyo, Deputy Resident Representative, United Nations Development Programme (UNDP), Venezuela; Dr. Milan Juranovic, Management Consultant, Venezuela; and Dr. Prom Panitchpakdi, Secretary-General, National Environment Board, Thailand.

Mr. Graham Brown, Chief Geologist, Australian Marine Resources Pty. Limited, gave valuable assistance with sections devoted to resource management and environmental impact assessment; and Mr. David J. Beale, Design and Engineering Consultant, exceeded filial duties in assisting with illustrations and expressing the desires of a younger generation for intelligent solutions.

Reading for this book covered thousands of publications and original manuscripts. I am indebted to many people who suggested the importance of certain publications which had interested them, some appear in relevant bibliographies.

Most of all I am indebted to Dr. S. W. Gentle, formerly Secretary and Permanent Head of my own erstwhile Ministry of Environment Control, New South Wales, Australia, now Special Adviser to the Minister for Lands, Sydney, for providing his notes on land-use planning, commenting on all draft sections of the book and reviewing the final draft for publication. I thank him particularly for strengthening my conviction that bureaucrats can *make things happen*, if time is taken to understand their systems.

Finally, I acknowledge indebtedness to those people who encouraged me to write this book. All were deeply concerned that many things they wanted done about the environment had stalled. I hope they find some satisfaction in knowing that I took their concern seriously.

(*Author's Note*: Quotations and footnotes have been kept to a minimum. However, in many cases readers will wish to pursue various matters further. A selected bibliography has therefore been included at the end of each chapter.)

CHAPTER 1

Introduction

"Out of your experience, why don't you write a book on environmental management?" Another book on the environment! Torrents of words about this popular theme keep printing presses racing! Some readers are bewitched; many bewildered; those not bothered are often simply bored! These were some of my reactions to the question. Colleagues persisted, and I succumbed.

Some may label my approach to resolving environmental problems as a "cook book". Frankly, the aim is to encourage policy, legislative, administrative and technical initiatives in pollution control, management of natural resources and environmental planning through the wise conservation of natural resources and effective use of total national resources, including people. To be practical the emphasis must be on ways to make this happen. Some recipes are included, so it *is* partly a cook book!

Attitudes to environmental management throughout the world leave much to be desired. They are generally apathetic, often pointless, sometimes thoughtless. Like all bad habits, these attitudes are usually deeply ingrained. So this book is designed to spur planners and decision makers (highly valuable resources) into taking intelligent account of the likely consequences of activities which may have an impact on the environment. Out of my experience, I have kept developing countries and their problems especially in mind.

This book is addressed particularly to these same busy people who possess the commendable ability to think, to work, to produce, to achieve. The survival of mankind in surroundings of improved quality depends on their efforts. The key is better management, through intelligent planning and decision making.

Management itself is a well-known word. *Environmental Management*, however, has been surrounded with an aura of mystery in which perfectly logical administrative actions and policies are usually lost in a sea of semantics.

"Environmental Management" does not mean "management of the environment". It *does* mean *management of activities within environmentally tolerable limits*—a simple truth too often evading the best-trained policy analysts and administrators.

There is no lack of environmental philosophy and dogma, laws and regulations, description and prescription. Despite all this, environmental degradation is a usual outcome of human activities.

Why? Among other reasons there is a lack of effective environmental management. Also, there is almost a complete lack of organized material related to the definition and practicabilities of fashioning a coherent environmental decision-making framework.

This book is addressed to this particular area of need in the hope that many more environmental managers can find a starting point to implement the policies handed to them by their governments. Even more important they should find avenues into which to channel badly needed initiatives in environmental management.

Environmental management is not solely a matter for government. Environmental deterioration can result from all human activities. Government must provide the leadership in a comprehensive environmental enhancement effort involving governments at all levels, the private sector and the community at large. As with most efforts to mobilize people it needs to be a careful blending of coercion and co-operation, education and incentive.

There are of course many ways, in theory and practice, of trying to achieve desirable results. The following pages explain a personal philosophy and approach, derived from experience in politics, government, business, technology, research and on professional field assignments relating to the environment.

My basic plan of attack is to outline the conflict between ecological and traditional philosophies of economic development. The application of technology to resources to create the products of modern society is described. Management skills are then explained in terms of an environmental philosophy. Managerial relationships to existing governmental systems are reviewed and related to the concept of considering the environment as an entity indivisible from these systems of public administration.

A practical way to investigate environmental initiatives is described. A process for analysing the environmental administration approach of individual states is proposed. Further consideration of the approach is then divided into natural subject area divisions of pollution control, natural resource management and environmental planning, with particular reference to economic development and land-use planning.

The "real world" of poverty, inadequate energy and insufficient food is reconciled with environmental concepts as a viable basis to assist in mobilizing food and energy resources to meet basic human needs and aspirations. Developmental mechanisms to make this reconciliation, including physical planning, research, technology assessment, technology transfer, training, education and communication are placed in context.

The threads of environmental management systems are drawn together, with the environmental administrative process shown to be cyclical in nature. A sample "action plan" is used to illustrate the ideas put forward.

So now to the first step, "environmental dilemmas".

CHAPTER 2

Environmental Dilemmas

"The real environmental issue is survival. The industrial society is destroying the world!" So say Doomsday prophets. "Governments ought to stop the rush to destruction before it's too late—probably it's too late anyway", they pontificate.

Doomsayers have always been vocal, readily attaching themselves to the fashionable issue of their particular day. The dilemma is: can such prophets be necessary? They are adept at stirring the populace out of cosy, complacent attitudes, but in so doing usually provoke over-reaction in those they claim to be saving. Like Aesop's character, they cry wolf too often and over all history have many times been confounded and had their causes eroded by human ingenuity.

Survival is, of course a very real issue and is mirrored in the whole ascent of mankind. Man has had to carve his niche on Earth. He has been an endangered species until recent times (and still is in some parts of the world). He continues to be a predator as well as a beneficiary of nature's largesse. Environmental hazards have constantly accompanied Man in his relatively short period on this planet. In this milieu the warnings of Doomsday have to be placed. Man is ever searching for new goals. The dilemma is always: will Man opt for short-term gains or accept the more difficult constraints of far-sighted actions?

Underlying environmental dilemmas is the fact that so much is written about the problems and so little about possible solutions. Solutions *are* possible. They are generally known in outline at least. But, remarkably, the institutional mechanisms to phase them into the human framework are often primitive. In parts of the world they are still crude and undeveloped.

Environmental problems do not disappear at the wave of a wand. Solutions always cost something in time, effort and money. The dilemma is: will those who clamour for, and benefit from, a cleaner environment with potable water, sanitation and ecological stability vehemently oppose paying their share of the cost?

In an evolutionary sense the developed countries are at the start of what might be called a "recycling phase". Their concerns are mainly with waging war on dirty air, polluted water, noise, congestion, outmoded housing, local shortages of energy. In contrast developing countries are in various stages of aspiring to this "pinnacle of success"—another dilemma!

Developing countries are primarily agriculturally or natural-resource based with small industrial sectors. Exploding populations and crowding into low-grade housing or shelter are often normal situations. Exploitive agriculture, pastoral pursuits, forestry, hunting, fishing or mining of natural resources have caused environmental damage, frequently on an increasing scale. Developing countries wish to get as quickly as possible to the living standards of developed countries. To do this their governments *must* accelerate the use of natural resources. The dilemma is: how to do this without getting into the environmental crisis situation of most developed countries? Lack of knowledge of the physical environment and its characteristics is not the basic reason for lack of progress in achieving a good standard of environmental management. Of much greater significance is the lack of means and experience at the institutional and organizational level of government within which decisions are made and enforced locally, nationally and internationally.

Existing legal and administrative structures to deal with what are known as *environmental problems* were usually implemented in earlier years to cope with the simpler requirements of societies with less intricate structures. *Ad hoc* amendments have been the usual reaction to increasing complexity. In this respect the dilemma is where to stop adjusting an apparatus of government and administration which served faithfully for so long. Obviously it is not coping effectively with present-day problems, many of which are visible.

The dilemma is: at what stage is it essential to revolutionize the methods of the past?

Expanding populations create a demand for living space. The space needed often overlies valuable community resources, perhaps fertile agricultural land, or brick-making clay, or gravel for concrete. The dilemma is, should a government clear the population from the area, or forgo the land and its resources and important food and bricks at a higher price? A more frequently occurring dilemma is for a government to find that it has valuable minerals within reserves set aside for nature conservation. Should it leave them sterilized within an area of land used by few of its people, or, should it utilize them to help raise living standards for everybody?

Governments, aided by every human and technical resource available to them, have to resolve such dilemmas. It is their function to arrive at practical solutions So let us look at the dilemma posed by the need to *use* the environment to develop rather than as merely a prop for survival.

Selected Bibliography

Marsh, George Perkins. *Man and Nature or, Physical Geography, as Modified by Human Action*. Harvard University Press, Cambridge, Mass., U.S.A. 1864.

Carson, Rachel. *Silent Spring*. Penguin Books Ltd, Middlesex, U.K. 1962.

Meadows, Donella H., *et al. The Limits of Growth: A Report for the Club of Rome's Project on the Predicament of Mankind*. Signet Books, New York. 1972.

Ehrlich, Paul R. *The Population Bomb*. Pan Books Ltd, London. 1971.

Toffler, Alvin. *Future Shock*. Pan Books Ltd, London. 1971.

Maddox, J. *The Doomsday Syndrome*. Macmillan, London. 1971.

Ward, Barbara, and Dubos, Rene. *Only One Earth: the Care and Maintenance of a Small Planet*. W. W. Norton & Co., Inc., New York. 1972.

United Nations. *Report on the United Nations Conference on the Human Environment (2–16 June 1972)*. Publication E.73.II.A.14.

Bronowski, J. *The Ascent of Man*. Little, Brown & Co., Boston, Mass., U.S.A. 1973.

Morgan, Elaine. *The Descent of Woman*. Corgi Books, London. 1973.

McHale, J. Mettale and Magda Cordell. *Human Requirements, Supply Levels and Outer Bounds: A Framework for Thinking about the Planetary Bargain*. The Aspen Institute for Humanistic Studies, Colorado, U.S.A. 1975.

Eckholm, Erik P. *Losing Ground: Environmental Stress and World Food Prospects.* W. W. Norton & Co., Inc., New York. 1976.

Mesarovic, Mihajlo, and Pestel, Eduard. *Mankind at the Turning Point: The Second Report to the Club of Rome.* Signet Books, New York. 1976.

United Nations Environment Programme. *UNITERRA (1977 Monthly Bulletins).* UNEP, Nairobi, Kenya.

Matthews, William H., (Ed.). *Outer Limits and Human Needs.* The Dag Hammarskjold Foundation, Uppsala, Sweden. 1976.

Meadows, D. L. and D. H. *Toward Global Equilibrium.* Wright Allen Press. Cambridge, Mass., U.S.A. 1973.

Crowe, Beryl L. *The Tragedy of the Commons Revisited, in the Politics of Ecosuicide.* Leslie L. Roos, Jr. (Ed.). Holt, Rinehart and Winston Inc., New York. 1971.

Kahn, Herman, *et al. The Next 200 Years, A Scenario for America and the World.* William Morrow & Co., Inc., New York. 1976.

CHAPTER 3

Development and the Environment

"We will ensure better living standards for all the people, all the time", say political propagandists. A few citizens respond, "But how can there be a good living environment if you promote economic development?"

One major conclusion of the 1972 United Nations Conference on the Human Environment was that there need be no inherent incompatibility between environment and development when they are seen in realistic long-term perspectives. This is reflected in the term "eco-development" coined by Maurice F. Strong, when he was Executive Director of the United Nations Environment Programme (UNEP), to describe the search for new and continuous harmony between development and the environment.

Each nation has its own unique individuality which is a combination of physical features, climate, resources, history, tradition, language, culture and state of development. Further developments should be in accordance with the "eco-development" concept, a key requirement being that economic growth should be adapted to local requirements, which will obviously vary from country to country. The concept also calls for the use of appropriate technology.

Every country has a scale of prosperity among its citizens, the disadvantaged being ill-clad, or badly housed, or susceptible to disease or malnutrition, or a combination of these. Development is essential so that their needs can have priority. It is possible to accelerate development within environmental limits that are tolerable to all sections of the nation. Governments by their nature, however, have to work at development within the constraints of local cultures, attitudes and aspirations. Developing and developed countries are not different in these respects. What does differ is the institutional and financial base from which future progress must be made. It is important to see environmental progress as an objective compatible with economic and social progress.

It is essential for administrators clearly to comprehend the difference between exploitation (in the sense of indiscriminate development) on one hand and preservation (sterilization) on the other, and also the middle course of conservation (wise use). The widely sought nexus between acceptable environmental use and satisfactory economic development is found only in wise use of resources. If ecologically based principles of development are used, economic progress can be sustained in perpetuity. If not, economic growth can lead to the collapse of the growth-sustaining resources. Realism lies in the ability of our systems to minimize environmental problems within the limits set by finite resources.

Natural resources are our environmental capital. As with any form of capital, poor management will lead to its dissipation while good husbandry will augment its usefulness. It is essential to realize that there are two classes of natural resources:

(a) Non-renewable
(b) Renewable

Non-renewable resources, such as mineral ore, can be consumed like most forms of capital to generate income. They may be part of a country's patrimony. Where natural resources are lacking, the local deficiency may be made up by imports, sometimes traded in exchange for other resources, often renewable ones.

Renewable resources are those which can be managed to generate income in perpetuity. Forests, fisheries and wildlife are examples. Soil is a renewable resource in part, expecially if reference is to its fertility. If the natural capital in the form of renewable resources is eroded, so is its capacity to generate a sustained income. Soil stripped of its nitrogen or phosphorus capital can no longer yield as much food. Forests depleted year by year lose their productivity. It should be clear that continued unwise use can make a renewable resource as valueless as a worked-out mine.

Unfortunately, the simple principle of matching available income to the resource capital (renewable and non-renewable) generating it, is not well enough understood in those levels of government concerned with environmental planning and administration. Often they need to have the theory put before them.

A strategy for better use of natural resources should take account of the inevitable consequences of their thoughtless depletion and exploitation. These consequences are expressed directly in lowered or degraded living standards for millions of people. Basic human needs for food, clothing, shelter, health and education greatly depend upon the quality of natural resource planning and management strategies.

Increasingly, the conventional strategy of economic development has concentrated on abundance and the use of high energy inputs to achieve better living standards. Material productivity has been accentuated whereas environmental concepts place the emphasis on development modes which can enhance human welfare in its broadest senses.

High energy styles of economic development generally have increased material productivity through intensified environmental degradation. Environmental concepts, when introduced, can lead to greater emphasis being placed on planning and managerial measures to forestall environmental and natural resource degradation.

There are obvious areas of conflict apparent between traditional economic development attitudes and current environmental approaches, especially in the short term. In a longer term perspective, however, it should be possible for the two modes to become complementary. For example, competing claims to use land for national heritage reservations as opposed to exploitive uses to satisfy short-term deficiencies should be soluble within a long-term philosophy. To achieve compatibility from the outset, planning and management activities need to focus on national environmental goals. To do this there must be an institutional framework capable of accepting environmental management systems.

Taking in physical, technological, ecological, economic, social cultural and political realities calls for a multi-disciplinary and multi-agency approach. Development and environmental concepts can then be made compatible, or at least, a reasoned dialogue can be maintained between conflicting interests, and about competing priorities. Unless this is done, inept planning and misuse of resources will be usual rather than exceptional. In its wake will come human misery and environmental degradation in the form of urban slums, dirty air, polluted waters, noise and natural resource deterioration. Future generations will find their options foreclosed.

In short, an environmental dimension needs to be injected into the planning and administration framework at national, regional and local levels. This calls for a higher order of management which is discussed in the following chapters.

Selected Bibliography

Hardin, G. *The Tragedy of the Commons.* Science, 162, 1243–48. 1968.

United Nations. *Development and the Environment.* Report and Working Papers of a Panel of Experts Convened by the Secretary-General of the United Nations Conference on the Human Environment (Founex, Switzerland, June 4–12, 1971), 1971.

Dasman, Raymond F., *et al. Ecological Principles for Economic Development.* John Wiley & Sons Ltd, London. 1973.

Sachs, Ignacy. *Eco-development.* Ecole des Hautes Etudes, Paris. 1973.

International Council of Scientific Unions Scientific Committee on Problems of the Environment. *Environment and Development.* Collected Papers, Summary Reports, and Recommendations, SCOPE/UNEP Symposium on Environmental Sciences in Developing Countries (Nairobi, February 11–23, 1973). SCOPE, Paris. 1974.

Poore, M.E.D. *A Conservation Viewpoint.* Proc. R. Soc., London. 339, 395–410. 1974.

Holmes, Nicholas, (Ed.). *Environment and the Industrial Society.* Hodder & Stoughton, London. 1976.

Leontief, Wassily. *The Future of the World Economy.* Oxford University Press, New York. 1977.

Herrera, Amilcar O., *et al. Catastrophe or New Society? A Latin American Model.* International Development Research Centre (IDRC-064e), Ottawa, Canada. 1976.

Dubos, Rene. *Symbiosis Between the Earth and Humankind Science.* Science, Vol. 193, No. 4252. 1976.

Tolba, Mostafa K. *Development Without Destruction.* Address to Chelsea College Staff, University of London. 1976.

United Nations. Documents bearing on the environment and development issued since the 1972 United Nations Conference on the Human Environment (UNCHE):

Declaration on the Establishment of a New International Economic Order (NIEO). Emphasizes the rational distribution and use of the world's resources. 1974.

Charter of Economic Rights and Duties of States. Stresses improving the lot of all people through the development of alternative patterns and styles of life, while ensuring "the protection, preservation, and enhancement of the environment". 1974.

Cocoyoc Declaration. Points to the need to meet basic human needs within the potentials and constraints of environmental systems and natural resources. 1974.

Lima Declaration and Plan of Action on Industrial Development and Co-operation. Recognizes that higher rates of industrial growth will have far-reaching repercussions on the physical and social environment. 1975.

CHAPTER 4

Resources, Technology and Management

"Science has made a mess of this planet: but given the money science can clean it up", the research expert confidently proclaimed. However, many environmental problems are not susceptible to purely technical solutions. For example, scientific and technological cleverness alone are inadequate to solve the problems of population growth, wasteful resource exploitation and pollution. These all have economic and social overtones. But knowledge of the combination of resources and technology is important in environmental problem solving.

Products of modern society come from the application of technology to resources. The impact of this process on the biosphere depends on the quality of the management applied to effect this combination, as illustrated schematically in Figure 1.

Primitive Man with his meagre wants and wastes existed largely in ecological balance with the surrounds. Early agricultural Man made greater impact on his habitat, particularly on soil resources. Also his more abundant food supply allowed the population to increase with resultant impact on the general environment.

Modern industrialized Man has reached a high level of affluence, especially in cities, where the residuals of daily living are seen as concentrations of litter, garbage, or rubbish. The tendency has been to use goods once only and throw away the remains, giving rise to the description "produce, consume and *dump*" society. Increasing affluence tends to translate into expanded productivity with increasing environmental degradation, as illustrated in Fig. 2. There is merit in scrutinizing life styles.

In both developing and developed countries there is obviously

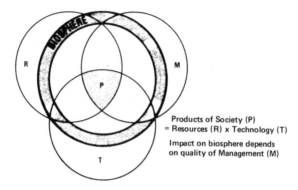

Fig. 1. Resources, Technology and Management Mix (*after Beale 1973*).

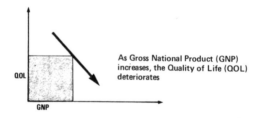

Fig. 2. "Produce, Consume and *Dump*" Society (*after Beale 1973*).

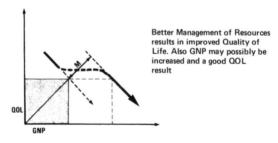

Fig. 3. "Produce, Consume and *Re-use*" Society (*after Beale 1973*).

need to achieve social goals by using resources in the best known ways. Also there is the need to curb excessive waste, that is, to avoid using more material than necessary to provide human fulfilment.

Fortunately, there is a noticeable trend towards increased recycling of potential pollutants. Steel, paper and glass are examples where residuals are often treated as resources instead of waste. Changing from the *dump* society to a "produce, consume and *re-use*" society, through better management of resources (including recycling) can permit both increased productivity and improved quality of life, as indicated diagrammatically in Fig. 3.

Sometimes technology is blamed for pollution when in fact the problem may arise from failure to take technology far enough. For example, primary sewage treatment may be provided where secondary or even tertiary treatment is desirable. In certain cases, there might be economic constraints, for example, the added anti-pollution cost might push a product above a competitive price. There may be social constraints, for example, jobs before cleanliness. However, the most usual constraint is an unwillingness, not an inability, to commit funds. This reluctance is often rooted in cultural attitudes, which by definition are historical, and the failure to comprehend the cost to the environment and the society it surrounds.

There is increasing recognition that whether a material is to be considered a valuable commodity or a pollutant to be discharged to the environment is often determined by prevailing prices. Changes in economic values to reflect economic and social costs of production, consumption and waste disposal can lead to a reduction in pollutant discharges to the surroundings and a more rational use of the environment.

Most processes to reduce pollutants in industrial discharges to very low levels consume substantial amounts of energy. The point can actually be reached at which those pollutants created during the generation of energy are being produced at a greater rate than the primary pollutants are being eliminated by the application of the extra energy.

In order to illustrate the concept that pollutants are misplaced resources, attention is drawn to the *materials balance* system as indi-

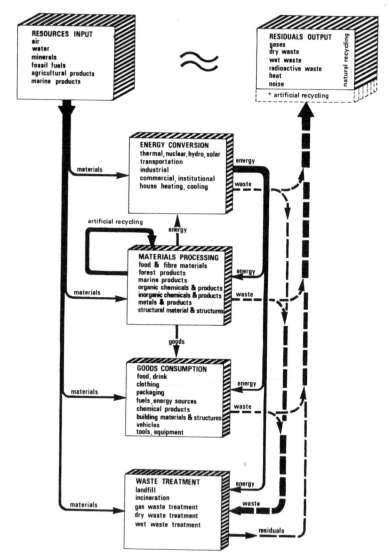

Fig. 4. Materials Balance System (*elaborated from Beale 1975*).

cated in Fig. 4. Inputs of resources are converted partly into goods and partly into residuals, *i.e.* potential pollutants. Most goods, after consumption, can also become residuals. Many inputs are discharged into the atmosphere in the form of gases from combustion of fossil fuels and animal respirations, and usually are not particularly harmful to natural systems. However, some of the remaining residual gases, dry solids and wet wastes tend to be potentially harmful.

The materials-balance view highlights the fact that the throughput of resources necessary for a given level of production decreases with increases in efficiency of energy conversion, materials usage, re-use and recycling. This concept is directly influenced by technical, economic and environmental factors.

A product may sometimes be manufactured by dissimilar processes and therefore result in extremely different residuals reaching the environment. Selection of a preferred system from the viewpoint of its potential to pollute should include selection of those residuals for which all impacts are minimal.

From Fig. 4 it can be deduced that a new plant may be built at a lower initial cost by incorporating only minimal pollution controls which may appear economic from the viewpoint of jobs and productivity created. Should the resulting residuals eventually harm a farming area downstream it must be realized that jobs and productivity had been achieved at the expense of the agricultural sector. Should pollution from the new plant degrade the water supply for a downstream town then the jobs and productivity it created may have to be offset by the cost of a town water treatment plant. Additionally, there could be social, health and amenity costs from any airborne residuals. As in any ecological system, the units are all interconnected and a materials-balance approach will indicate potential gains and losses. Balancing gains and losses is the manager's job. It is essential therefore to examine how managerial skills relate to environmental management and administration. Success will largely depend on those skills.

Selected Bibliography

Kneese, V., *et al.*, *Economics and the Environment: A Materials Balance Approach.* Resources for the Future. Washington D.C., U.S.A. 1970.

Bohn, P., and Kneese, V. (Ed.). *The Economics of the Environment.* Papers from Four Nations. Resources for the Future. Washington D.C., U.S.A. 1971.

Sachs, Ignacy. *La Science, facteur de progress ou obstacle en development due Tiers Monde?* Problemes Economiques, No. 1253. Paris. 1972.

Hamilton, David. *Technology, Man and the Environment.* Faber & Faber Ltd, London. 1973.

Jequier, Nicholas (Ed.). *Appropriate Technology: Problems and Promises.* OECD, Paris. 1976.

CHAPTER 5

Managerial Skills and the Environment

"The plans were perfect," the administrative head said ruefully, "but the programme hasn't worked out. Worse still—we've been criticised for bad management."

Planning and managerial skills are not identical. Failure is simply due in many cases to lack of managerial skill. Management takes a policy line handed to it and incorporates planning and programming. Included in this are assignments of responsibility, marshalling of resources (human and physical), setting priorities, co-ordination and control of operations, review of performance (feedback), and subsequent resetting of objectives as the need is seen.

Man has always been a manager. Without managing to achieve a reasonable level of harmony with nature he would not have survived. Ingenuity has been used to gain a very considerable degree of mastery over the environment. Where this "mastery" has resulted in an overloading of his surroundings Man has been evicted or pre-empted by nature during the course of his rise as a species.

In modern times, life-support systems, particularly those in bigger cities, insulate Man increasingly from natural forces—or so mankind likes to think. Despite all his managerial skills, earthquakes, tidal waves, volcanic eruptions, cyclones, floods, droughts, plagues and epidemics constantly remind him of his precarious hold. Natural impacts have been heightened and intensified by environmental mismanagement—destruction of water catchments and vegetation, alteration of natural coastal barriers, dirtying of air and waters, and so on. The call is to manage rehabilitation of degraded environments, to reduce the strain on local, regional and global environments.

The most utilized environments are remarkably resilient but impacts on them must be kept within the limits of ecosystem stability. Only if managerial decisions are made with adequate thought for the fact that there *is* an environment, and that it has definite capabilities and capacities, can there be any certainty of a reasonable measure of stability. Just as a good housewife has over time developed her household levels of competent performance through management within physical, financial and cultural constraints, so must planners and administrators aim their efforts at better housekeeping of the environment.

Environmental management is not "management of the environment"—it is *management of activities within tolerable constraints imposed by the environment itself, and with full consideration of ecological factors.* The objective is to meet basic human needs within the potentials and constraints of environmental systems.

Environmental management introduces three new dimensions into traditional socio-economic development:

(*a*) it broadens the concept in scope, to include development and enhancement of *environmental quality;*
(*b*) it extends the concept in time, to include *sustainable* long-term feasibility; and
(*c*) it assesses the *costs* to society and the environment in achieving the desired balance between (*a*) and (*b*).

Managerial skills are usually available but not always used because environmental information is not often analysed into forms useful to managers. Sometimes resources to implement management decisions are not supplied, or the political will to grapple with other than rhetoric is lacking. Also, outmoded legal, administrative and technical arrangements may hinder environmental initiatives. The longer-term and trans-sectoral nature of environmental management *is* difficult to respond to, but the challenge is usually interesting and fulfilling to managers.

Managerial relationships to existing governmental systems are reviewed in the next chapter.

Selected Bibliography

Brubaker, Sterling. *To Live on Earth.* Resources for the Future, Inc., the Johns Hopkins University Press, Baltimore, Maryland, U.S.A. 1972.

Garlauskas, A. B. *Conceptual Framework of Environmental Management.* Journal of Environmental Management. pp. 185–203 (3, 1975).

Matthews, William H., *et al. Resource Materials for Environmental Management and Education.* The M.I.T. Press, Cambridge, Mass., U.S.A. 1976.

Centre d'Etudes Industrielles. *International Programme in Environmental Management Education* (IPEME). Annual Report and Workshops. Geneva, Switzerland. 1977.

Beale, J. G. *Draft Guide to Environment Protection and Management. A basis for National Environment Initiatives.* Prepared for discussions with the United Nations Environment Programme. UNEP, Nairobi, Kenya. 1975.

CHAPTER 6

Governmental Systems

1. Governmental Relationships

"I can't understand it. The 'Chief Executive' announced the project as top priority, and not a thing has happened." Not only the ordinary citizen expresses these sentiments. Elitists—scientists, engineers, architects, planners, often ponder the same point. Mostly they have not appreciated the workings of governmental machinery. Even more usually they exhibit apathy about the workings of government until it fails to deliver the goods. The following comments may help to set the scene for those who believe that a government should always respond instantly.

Governments publish details of their systems and of course these vary greatly. Comparisons between systems of government can be obtained from directories.* To simplify further comment, Fig. 5 shows the commonest governmental relationship.

2. Government

a. Constitution

Governments of countries are seen in many forms. Those falling into the categories of monarchies, republics and presidencies are

*One such concise, up-to-date view can be obtained from *The International Year Book and Statesman's Who's Who*, Kelly's Directories Ltd, Kingston-upon-Thames, Surrey.

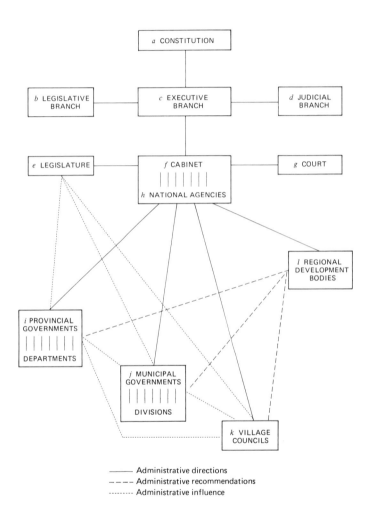

Fig. 5. Some Common Governmental Relationships (schematic).

mostly governed under constitutions. Those with martial law are often governed by "ruler" decrees which also provide a framework for the governmental system.

A national Constitution (*a*) defines in broad outline what the three branches of government—legislative (*b*), executive (*c*) and judicial (*d*)—can do. The Constitution often provides a useful lead to the environmental aspirations of the inhabitants of a country, for example, Article 77 of the 1974 Constitution of the Kingdom of Thailand proclaims, "The State should maintain and preserve the balance of the environment and natural beauty, including forests, watersheds, waterways and territorial waters."

Constitutions may also lay down the more general powers of lower levels of government to make specific detailed laws and regulations. In certain respects, these governmental levels are closer than the national government to many environmental problems. The 1961 Venezuelan Constitution for example defines a Municipality as the *primary political unit*. It places on the 700 municipalities powers pertaining to "urbanization, supplies, circulation, culture, sanitation, social assistance, credit, popular institutes, tourism and police".

b. Legislature

Under most constitutions the seat of legislative power is a national assembly. Usually it is a body of elected representatives but sometimes they are appointed. The Constitution defines the powers of the Legislature (*e*) to make detailed laws.

Countries under martial law carry out the legislative function by decrees issued under the authority of the Head of the Government. A chief executive may be assisted in this by a small appointed national council.

Individual representatives of an elected national assembly, particularly if it is based on a popular electoral system, can be highly sensitive to a ground swell of public opinion. "Environmentalists" should be aware, however, that this type of legislative system is inherently complicated and slow-moving. Such machinery is unlikely to react speedily to suit their whims. Intelligent and persistent efforts are required to gain reforms such as a comprehensive national environmental management law, laws in specific areas like air, water and noise pollution or amendments to strengthen existing legislation on water, soil, forests, mineral and marine resources, and planning.

Where the legislative powers are vested in the Head of the Government it is possible for a decree to be issued promptly. However "environmentalists" should realize that with or without an appointed national council, this legislative process can often be tardy and less sensitive to their aspirations.

Where there are two or more levels of government the national legislature usually has constitutional power to make laws binding on them. This can be important because a nationally enacted law binding on a local government can be a useful environmental tool. In Sri Lanka, for example, the First Schedule of the national 1956 Town and Country Planning Ordinance provides, among other things, for the control of land use, roads, structures, public services (including drainage, sewerage, refuse, waste disposal) and nuisances; the preservation of views, prospects and features of natural beauty; the planting and preservation of vegetation. It should be apparent that legislatures at the lower levels also can have important environmental powers in their own rights.

c. Executive

The structure of government may include as Head of State a Monarch or President although in many cases this function is merely symbolic. A presidential call to a nation for a better environmental attitude could influence the community at large and in this regard a message from a symbolic Head of State often can be potent.

In democracies, the supreme Executive arm of government embodies the principle of responsible Cabinet government. In practice, where governments are based essentially on the British system, policy is decided by a committee of Ministers of State under the chairmanship of the Prime Minister, called a Cabinet (*f*), as for example in the United Kingdom itself. In some instances this type of executive body is a group of representatives chosen entirely from the majority in the national assembly, as in Australia. In other cases it may be a group appointed by the directly elected President of the country, as in the U.S.A.

Under martial law the Head of the Government may be the sole ruler of the country, embodying legislative, executive and judicial powers. Sometimes this power is shared between the members of a revolutionary or national committee.

No matter what form a supreme executive may take, "environmentalists" should appreciate that this body will be under extreme pressure to establish policies which fit in with its concept of the most pressing national goals, for example, defence, food, housing, jobs. It is accustomed to dealing in hard facts and those wishing to effect a shift in policy must serve up their proposals in a form which indicates that they account for national priorities, are well researched, consistent with established facts, and are both technically and politically feasible.

d. Judiciary

Constitutions usually vest the judicial power of government in a supreme Court (g).

It is important to note that while a constitution gives an outline of government, the decisions of the Court may determine much of the detail of the day-to-day position. These decisions can also serve to update the Constitution relative to present-day needs. Thus, the U.S. Constitution is 200 years old, but is kept surprisingly relevant by a continuing Supreme Court review of its operation. "Environmentalists" should note this because in most countries current interpretations of laws and their penalties can be important factors in moves for environmental enhancement.

Where there is martial law, the Court is often permitted to determine many details of the day-to-day running of the country under older legislation, amended from time to time under decrees issued by the Head of the Government. In the Philippines, for example, there are Commonwealth Acts, Republic Acts, Presidential Decrees and Presidential Letters of Instruction, all serving to assist the Court's interpretation of the law.

Courts at lower levels often have important environmental control powers to discharge. For this reason it should be appreciated that lower jurisdictions usually have power over areas of local government within which substantial environmental damage can, and does in fact occur; examples are inadequate sanitation and unsuitable building development.

3. National Objectives

a. Stated or Unstated

Most national constitutions outline broad national objectives. Some constitutions state an environmental objective, as in Thailand's Articles 77 and 93. Others are silent in a directive sense, but they can imply an environmental object. For example, the 1972 Sri Lankan Constitution, Chapter V—Principles of State Policy, "which shall guide the making of laws and the government of Sri Lanka", includes in Section 16 (2) (g) the pledge to achieve "the organization of society to enable the full flowering of human capacity both individually and collectively in the pursuit of the good life".

An environmental objective is expressed in the preamble to the 1973 Constitution of the Republic of the Philippines, "We, the sovereign Filipino people, imploring the aid of Divine Providence, in order to establish a Government that shall embody our ideals, promote the general welfare, *conserve and develop the patrimony of the Nation*, and secure to ourselves and our posterity the blessings of democracy under a regime of justice, peace, liberty, and equality, do ordain and promulgate this Constitution."

Rather than appearing in the Constitution, environmental objectives are sometimes set out in specific laws and decrees, within constitutional limits, which legislate the policy aims of a government. The 1969 U.S. National Environmental Policy Act (NEPA), the Thailand 1975 Law on the Promotion and Protection of the Quality of the National Environment, and the Philippine 1976 Presidential Decree creating the Human Settlements Commission, are all examples of laws outlining national objectives.

Some national objectives, such as those relating to defence and employment, are usually well understood by the community. Often however the national stance on environmental matters is indefinite or unstated. There is scattered mention in numerous laws of small aspects taken out of the whole environmental context. In place of understanding there is national apathy on a vital matter.

b. Planned

In contrast to those with unscheduled statements of environmental objectives, many nations, especially developing countries, do have planned objectives. They prepare national development plans, for example the Venezuelan 4th Plan of the Nation (1970–75). Plans of this type are important. Even when they have had to be amended, or when the targets were not reached, they have influenced economic trends and, by this route, daily life. To some degree they have imposed environmental controls.

Most such plans are primarily economic development plans although recently there has been a trend toward greater "social" content. The Third Economic and Social Development Plan (1972–76) of Thailand strategies include "greater emphasis on social development".

There is an opportunity in this area for "environmentalists" to work diligently for an increase in the "environmental" content. A step along this path is seen in The Fourth Five-Year Plan (1977–1981) of Thailand, principally because the Government set out to make the Plan a vehicle for implementing its objectives. A new development strategy is "To improve the management of basic resources and rehabilitate environmental conditions."

In some countries an associated objective of interest may be land-use planning and here again there is an opportunity to enlarge the environmental input to comprehensive national development plans of this type. However, traditional land ownership patterns may hinder the attainment of national land-use planning or environmental goals.

c. Unplanned

In further contrast to overtly stated national environmental objectives as discussed above, there is a further group of countries, especially developed countries, without specific national plans. Others only have partial or fragmented planning. At the same time a careful look at the overall framework is certain to reveal some fairly clear objectives. Sometimes environmental objectives are obscure or diffuse and need precise definition if anything comprehensive is to be achieved.

In such countries, it is traditional for governmental agencies and large-scale private entrepreneurs to have individual development plans which might cover in part similar fields of endeavour. The Executive branch of government has in these cases an opportunity to play a co-ordinating role and it is here that an environmental input can be introduced. Such action is not, however, in the same directive category as the planning which is possible where more comprehensive national plans exist.

Some developed countries like the U.S.A. and Australia, which have unplanned economies, may spell out national objectives through legislation and this can influence unplanned sectors. For example, the 1969 U.S. National Environmental Policy Act (NEPA) is advisory in nature but it influences economic growth through its very strong effect on industrial location planning, investment levels, stratification of industrial processing and so on. In the Australian federation, environmental objectives are set out in a rather loose and varying mixture of Federal and State policies and laws.

4. Administration

a. Centralized

Under the Executive, governmental administration is usually divided into a number of sectoral National Agencies (*h*) designed to carry out specific tasks, for example, agriculture, health, education.

Some countries have highly centralized forms of administration dominated by the national agencies. This organization of agencies tends to provide strong central control which can promptly issue directives in line with the wishes of the national executive. In environmental areas of interest the administration then tends to be made up of single-mission agencies co-ordinated only by regular meetings of the political representatives responsible for each agency, as in the cabinet system.

Division into specialist areas served governments reasonably well in the past. The system may have particular advantages in times of emergency. In today's world, however, the total governmental structure may not be adequately responsive to the changing aspirations of the people on complex matters like environmental quality, unless vertical communication is very effective. Similarly important areas of environmental administration may suffer because their political representatives do not possess sufficient ranking to press reforms adequately when reforms are in fact urgently needed.

b. Decentralized

The majority of countries have decentralized forms of government. They may have national or federal systems with provincial, municipal and village governments (i, j, k).

The Republic of the Philippines has national, provincial, municipal and village levels of government. Australia has a Commonwealth Government and six State Governments; that is, seven governments, to share the national powers, and it also has over 1000 municipal and rural councils.

Countries with decentralized administrations usually have a range of national agencies with sectoral responsibilities. Additionally, however, there will be divisions of administrative power at lower levels within agencies and departments responsible for specific duties. From an environmental viewpoint a usual consequence is some duplication of functions.

Problems may also arise where specialist national, provincial and municipal agencies and village councils are in conflict on a particular issue, or often worse, parts of the issue. Notwithstanding autonomy granted to individual regulatory agencies, public enterprises and *ad hoc* bodies, they are not freed of responsibility to operate within the broad policy of the government.

A decentralized system may respond slowly to the directives of the national government. However, the total national governmental structure may work better at lower governmental levels, especially at the grass roots level. An important proviso is that there be reasonably efficient vertical and horizontal communication. People accustomed to these forms of local-level government usually believe that their tax levies are spent most efficiently by the level of government closest to their own communal supervision. The environment may also fare better. However, much depends on having adequate provision to notify intent, such as the intentions of government and private developers to change land use, establish industry, or alter established management practices, or allow public participation.

c. Regional

There are almost universally expressed difficulties about the co-ordination of governmental structures at all levels. One trend has been to correct the position by establishing regional administrations. Some of these have executive powers while others have only advisory functions.

Some regional bodies are specific-purpose extensions of the national government, for example, economic development and regional planning bodies, in fact becoming virtually a further level of government. Sri Lanka has District Government Agents as direct decentralized representatives of the national Executive. The Philippines has specific-purpose Regional Development Councils operating under The National Economic Development Authority. Venezuela has Regional Corporations which are primarily economic development bodies.

Environmental managers should realize that this trend to regional administration can provide fertile ground for the seeding of environmental approaches to planning and development. It is a most effective level to introduce ideas and is possibly the level offering the best compromise between co-ordination of effort by various agencies and successful implementation of ideas.

5. Environmental Administration

a. The Influence of International Concern

Over the last decade there has been an increasing tendency for nations to exchange information on their national approaches towards environmental management and control. The 1972 Stockholm Conference on the Human Environment truly internationalized the information flow. There was a very specific interest in institutional arrangements as adopted by various nations. Since then the International Referral System (IRS) has assisted the flow.

Naturally enough, institutional systems of administration will differ considerably. Despite differences in national infrastructures there has been a remarkable tendency, not always wisely considered, to copy the systems of those nations which acted first. National challenges and national mores towards the environment vary considerably with the result that "blueprint" solutions appropriate to, say, the Anglo-Saxon world, cannot always be expected to work efficiently in the Latin world.

This is not to say that there has not been experimentation. The following sections indicate the wide range of tested ideas with comment on the more common systems.

b. Cabinet or Council of Ministers

Some governments prefer to deal with significant issues at the most senior Executive level, for example, meetings of the Cabinet or Council of Ministers. The view is that Ministers or Secretaries of State will carry out their tasks responsibly and that any dispute between them can be resolved as a political problem at this level.

Sometimes this idea is extended to the appointment of a sectoral Cabinet Subcommittee on the Environment. Members are the Ministers whose administrations are most concerned with environmental matters such as those with responsibilities for health, agriculture, natural resources and industry. In Venezuela in 1974 the Council of Ministers established an Inter-Ministerial Commission for Environment.

Basically, the arrangement has the advantage that it does lead to decision. Issues can be forced and the decision itself can be used with the authority of the elite group making it. On the debit side it is possible to obtain very poor decisions in this manner, with too little factual information and too little time allocated to considering all aspects.

The notion can be further expanded by adding some senior agency executives to the ministerial subcommittee. This arrangement was used in Thailand in 1974. In 1975 the idea was elaborated through legislation into the National Environment Board (NEB) by adding-in a further group of experts drawn from outside the Government.

c. Existing Agencies

As noted earlier, many governments administer environmental problems through traditional national agencies, for example, departments of health, agriculture, industry, water, forests, public works, transport. These governments expect specialized agencies, some having environmental components, to carry out their duties efficiently within their statutory charters. In so doing, governments argue that the agencies will take care of their particular portions of the total environment problem.

It is customary for government agencies to deal with matters beyond their charters in times of emergency. So, some governments are attracted to operating existing agencies under directions from the chief executive of the nation on environmental issues.

There are some advantages to be seen in a government merely directing existing agencies to take account of the environment in their individual activities. A major disadvantage is that piecemeal policies, while appearing to be individually sound to single mission agencies, may later prove collectively harmful to the environment. Almost always there is duplication of effort with resultant disputes between agencies. Sometimes, however, this can force corrective action.

The Philippine government dealt with this problem in 1976 by establishing an Inter-Agency Environmental Committee. In 1974 the Government of Thailand dealt with the situation in a more extended way. Its Inter-Agency Environmental Committee included some people outside of the central government administration. The Government of Venezuela in 1975 took action on a different way by using its national planning agency (CORDIPLAN) to secure a co-ordinated agency approach.

d. Special Ministers and Agencies

Increasingly governments have tended to appoint special Ministers for Environment, and special Departments of Environment, as in the United Kingdom. Sometimes this is referred to as the "environmental umbrella" approach.

At times the ministerial responsibility has been confined to a limited special grouping, examples being natural resources management groups, resource conservation groups (water, soil, forests, fisheries) or pollution control groups (air, water, noise).

In other approaches the specialized responsibility has been discharged through combining existing functions, for example, planning and environment administrations. In the State of New South Wales, Australia, there is a Planning and Environment Commission, while another State, Victoria, combines natural resource and land allocation agencies. To illustrate how variable the approach can be, a further State within the Australian federation, South Australia, after combining planning and environment administration for a period of some years decided eventually that less conflicts in administration resulted with the roles divorced.

Where there is ministerial responsibility solely for "the environment", the design of the agency for this has varied considerably. From a small advisory group of multi-disciplinary specialists to a huge department combining special environmental responsibilities with the traditional administration of areas such as transport and local government as encompassed by the U.K Department of Environment.

Some governments have preferred to establish various special agencies. The U.S. Council on Environmental Quality is a small group advising the President. In contrast the National Environment Board in Thailand and the Venezuelan National Council on Environment are both large groups comprising ministers, agency executives and outside representatives presided over by a Minister.

At a cursory glance the establishment of a major environment agency appears to be an attractive proposition. In the past, when it has been possible to define a specific area of pressing governmental concern, the common practice has been for governments to establish a new single mission agency, for example, health, agriculture, education. There are, however, difficulties in applying this traditional approach because environmental considerations permeate all agencies.

Numerous governmental agencies have specific functions and activities related to environmental protection and management. Assembling the environmental components from these agencies to make a major environment agency tends to provide strong centralized control.

A disadvantage of this design can be its large unwieldy nature. This has been recognized in the reduction in the size and scope of the huge U.K. Department of Environment. Another disadvantage is the removal of environmental responsibility from the decentralized action-oriented agencies, which are much closer to the threatened environment. The result is usually a less effective attack on environmental problems due to conflicts which arise with other strong single-mission agencies. There is also lessened drive at lower governmental levels.

e. Gathering together the best available scientific and technological expertise in a national group to provide advice to the government is also attractive. For example, in 1974, Poland established The Research Institute on Environmental Development—a consolidation of four former Research Institutes in some specialized fields of environmental planning, design and management. The brief on the Institute states the following:

The Institute reports to the Ministry of Land Economy and Environmental Protection and its main responsibility is to elaborate scientific and intellectual foundations for the Ministry's activities. In addition, the Institute performs part of its research works as a component of the research programme of the Polish Academy of Sciences. Further, it conducts the applied research commissioned by various levels of local subsidiaries which answer these local/regional specialized needs and conditions. Finally, the Institute conducts training and "refreshment" courses for its own and for its national-wide professional staff.

The Institute performs basic scientific research, applied research, development of research results and conclusions, and above that conducts some planning, design and implementation activities of pilot and demonstration projects.

There are advantages to be seen in the idea of high level technical thought flowing into high level administration. Also there are advantages at times in having discussions on important environmental problems in an academic atmosphere so that principles rather than specific problems are elaborated.

The obvious disadvantage can be that experts in their routine activities are sometimes remote from the real world in which practical political and administrative decisions are essential. Another disadvantage is that discussions in the rarefied atmosphere of a scientific council tend to be removed from the needs of action-oriented sectors of government. As a result scientific approaches to problems tend to be emphasized instead of the more political approach needed in practical environmental management.

f. Links to Planning and Plans

In contrast with using functional administrative units in isolation, governments have less often linked environmental administration to development planning and plans.

In some cases the national economic planning authority has been given an environmental unit. The idea is that a small multi-disciplinary group can introduce an environmental segment into the national economic plan. This is the position in the Philippines where the National Economic Authority now includes a small environmental unit. The National Economic and Social Development Board of Thailand also has a small unit which contributed to the environmental content of the Fourth Five-Year Plan.

In other cases an environmental thrust is provided through a unit within the regional planning organization. In Venezuela, for example, in 1975, the National Spatial-Regional Planning Division of CORDIPLAN appointed an Environment Co-ordination Unit which acted to provide the environmental input.

6. Regulatory Areas

The environment is composed of numerous subsystems which operate interdependently. Man is served by all systems and in making use of them alters or impairs their functioning. Not least of the subsystems is the organization of people themselves. Figure 6 shows schematically some simpler environmental interactions.

The growing complexity of human organization and human activities has given rise to equally complex environmental problems. Human settlements, rural and agricultural activities, industrialization, transportation and recreational demands are all areas where policies with an environmental outreach need to be implemented.

For the purpose of regulation it is useful to distinguish three major areas of environmental administration, namely:

• Pollution control
• Natural resources management
• Environmental planning

Most programmes or methods can be fitted within these categories which in turn can have the effect of concentrating action within what are otherwise fragmented sections in the attack on environmental degradation.

Pollution Control

Pollution in many forms has always attended human activities. Prior to the Industrial Revolution its onset was almost always related to increasing density of human settlement. The salting of ancient irrigation area soils, the disease-producing potential of local water supplies and the clogging of waterways by eutrophication are all facets of pollution induced by incremental activities which in the final event overwhelmed natural counteractive mechanisms.

Modern industrial pollution adds a further dimension to regulatory activity. In some cases it accelerates natural processes beyond the capacity of the environment to absorb the residuals. In other cases it adds to the natural environment materials for which no natural purifying mechanisms have evolved and which, if left unmanaged, eventually affect the health of the human population.

Pollution control therefore needs to ensure that natural purification systems are not overloaded or poisoned and that effective man-made systems of pollution control are installed where natural or synthetic

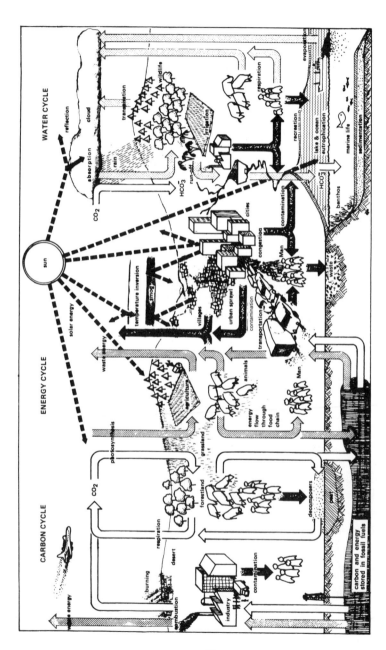

Fig. 6. Some Environmental Interactions (schematic).

38

pollutants cannot be tolerated or naturally processed by the environment to which they are discharged. These comments are expanded in Chap. 10.

Natural Resource Management

Resource management is primarily concerned with achieving an optimum allocation of resources including land, natural features, capital and labour. It is also concerned with conserving biological, mineral and energy resources to ensure adequate supplies for future needs.

Where an environmental programme is fully operational, the regulation of resource management, particularly natural resources, becomes an important component. Pollution control in itself diverts residual resources such as energy or municipal waste, or eroding soil, or otherwise derelict land or water resources to more valuable employment. Effectively managed resources rarely contribute significantly to pollution. They can also be subject to environmental planning controls. Collection of wastes can be a bonus. Sulphur, for example, is often valuable enough to justify considerable regulation to prevent its emission from smoke stacks. Recovered, it becomes a resource once more, rather than a pollutant.

Increasing population and urbanization accelerate pressures for land development. This imposes competing demands for retention and use of land resources for such purposes as conservation, agriculture, urban development, major projects, recreation and tourism. Land capability assessments can be a regulatory basis for rationalizing these competing demands in an efficient and environmentally sensitive manner. Natural resources management is discussed in greater detail in Chap. 11.

Environmental Planning

"Prevention is better than cure", and planning with proper account for the environment is a regulatory means of balancing resource management and resource allocation against the tendency to exploit resources needlessly, carelessly or inadvisedly for immediate gain. Environmental development planning needs to ensure that society receives the benefits but at the same time has its environmental resources preserved for future use.

Whereas pollution control is the present task, environmental development planning is the forward step taken to mitigate future pollution. As an example, new agricultural developments could be prohibited on very steep slopes where consequent accelerated soil erosion is likely to pollute downstream waters, harm town water supplies and fisheries, and in the process destroy the soil resource.

Environmental development planning refers to human settlements as well as natural environments. It also takes into account ecological, economic, technical and the social inputs to planning. It is the essence of "eco-development".

Environmental development planning both relies on, and provides the regulatory mechanism for integrating and co-ordinating special purpose approaches with the activities of developers, public and private. Unlike pollution control, which is remedial in nature, and natural resources management, which is mission-oriented, environmental development planning takes new initiatives and provides the incentives for multi-purpose government and community objectives. Environmental planning is discussed more extensively in Chap. 12.

7. Regulatory Methods

a. National Level

Governments deal with environmental matters through a variety of regulatory methods—policy, law, regulation, local rules and regional plans. Some parts of the environment such as water, sewage and waste, have been regulated since the early days of civilization. Existing laws can assist environmental management.

To this day almost all countries have laws on health, hygiene, human waste and garbage. Some now have comprehensive legal measures on the environment, but these are generally broad-based and organic in nature, as are the 1969 U.S. National Environmental Policy Act (NEPA), the 1975 Thailand Law on the Promotion and

Protection of the Quality of the National Environment, and the 1976 Venezuelan Organic Law on the Environment.

A number of countries now have sectoral laws about pollution: clean water, clean air, noise abatement. In many cases there are specific planning, resource, conservation and funding laws.

b. Regional Level

Some countries have developed regional standards to regulate effluents and emissions. These are usually in the form of regulations under national laws relating to such matters as discharges into streams or emissions from motor vehicles, a comprehensive example being the elaboration of Federal laws within the State of California.

Sometimes regional regulations will apply to a "city state", as happens in the cases of the cities of Metro-Manila, Caracas or Los Angeles.

A growing tendency is to develop regional environmental standards and regulations on a "basin" basis, that is, to control activities in an entire river or drainage basis unit. In this way, the quality of air and water can be monitored and pollution traced to its individual sources where controls can be implemented.

c. Local Level

Usually there are environmentally oriented ordinances and regulations covering municipalities, rural areas and villages. They cover such areas as the control of building, housing standards, licensing of noxious trades, drinking water quality and waste disposal.

These local laws are most often administered by the various sub-regional units of government. They are very important because the authorities administering them are closest to the threatened environment. Even more important these regulatory authorities usually are the most susceptible to subverting the aims of environmental legislation. They are also important in signalling to environmental managers the practicality of laws, ordinances and regulations. if certain laws are being unusually subverted it is essential to assess their efficiency either as *law*, or as *enforceable law*.

Selected Bibliography

Kelly's Directories Ltd. *The International Year Book and Statemen's Who's Who.* Kingston upon Thames, Surrey, U.K. 1977.

Constitution of the Kingdom of Thailand. 1974.

     Article 77 (translation). "The State should maintain and preserve the balance of the environment and natural beauty, including forests, watersheds, waterways and territorial waters."

     Article 93 (translation). "The State should maintain and preserve the environment in a clean condition and eradicate any pollution which is harmful to the welfare and health of the people."

Constitution of the Republic of Venezuela. 1961. Extracts (translation). The *"Municipality"* is the *"primary political unit"* and it is *"autonomous"* within the national organization. It has powers pertaining to *"urbanization, supplies, circulation, culture, sanitation, social assistance, credit, popular institutes, tourism and police."*

Republican Constitution of Sri Lanka. 1972. Chapter V—Principles of State Policy, "which shall guide the making of laws and the governance of Sri Lanka," includes in Section 16(2)(g) the pledge to achieve the objective of *"the organization of society to enable the full flowering of human capacity both individually and collectively in the pursuit of the good life."*

Constitution of the Republic of the Philippines. 1973. The preamble states, "We, the sovereign Filipino people, imploring the aid of Divine Providence, in order to establish a Government that shall embody our ideals, promote the general welfare, *conserve and develop the patrimony of our Nation,* and secure to ourselves and our posterity the blessings of democracy under a regime of justice, peace, liberty, and equality, do order and promulgate this Constitution."

Town and Country Planning Ordinance. 1947. (1956 Revision). First Schedule. Sri Lankan Legislative Enactment.

The National Environmental Policy Act (NEPA), U.S.A. Legislative Enactment. 1969.

Law on the Promotion and Protection of the Quality of the National Environment (translation). Thailand Legislative Enactment. 1975.

Organic Law of the Environment. Venezuelan Legislative Enactment. 1976.

Presidential Decree No. 933 Creating the Human Settlements Commission. The Philippines. 1976.

Office of the President, Caracas. *4th Plan of the Nation* (1970–75). Venezuela. 1970.

Office of the President, Caracas. *5th Plan of the Nation* (1975–80). Venezuela. 1975.

Office of the Prime Minister, Bangkok. *The Third Economic and Social Development Plan* (1972–76). Thailand. 1972.

Office of the Prime Minister, Bangkok. *The Fourth Five-Year Plan* (1977–1981). Thailand. 1977.

Office of the President, Manila. *Four-Year Development Plan* (1974–77). The Philippines. 1974.

Office of the Prime Minister, Colombo. *The Five-Year Plan* (1972–76). Sri Lanka. 1971.

Office of the Prime Minister, Colombo. *Review of The Five-Year Plan and Revised Development Programmes* (1975–77). Sri Lanka. 1975.

Instytut Ksztaltowania Srodowiska. *Brief on the Research Institute on Environmental Development.* Warsaw, Poland. 1974.

Cordiplan. *National System for Co-ordinating Environmental Planning and Administration.* Caracas, Venezuela. 1975.

Presidential Office on Reorganization. *Organization Charts for Government Agencies.* Manila, The Philippines. 1976.

National Institute of Development Administration. *The Government Organization Charts.* Research Centre, NIDA, Bangkok, Thailand. 1973.

Office of the President. *Government Organization Charts.* Caracas, Venezuela. 1975.

National Environment Board. *Office of the National Environment Board.* Bangkok, Thailand. 1976.

Research Management Centre. *Governmental Administration (Draft).* Colombo, Sri Lanka. 1976.

Inter-Agency Committee on Environmental Protection. *Report for the President on Environmental Protection.* Manila, The Philippines. 1976.

Mendis, M. W. J. G. *Local Government in Sri Lanka.* Colombo. 1976.

President of Venezuela. *First Message of the President of the Republic to the National Congress.* Section 19. *Environment.* 1975.

A Sub-Committee in Collaboration with the National Science Council. *Environmental Management in Sri Lanka.* Government Publications Bureau, Colombo. 1973. (Published 1976).

Department of Environment. *D.O.E. and Its Work.* A factual note about the functions of the Department of Environment. London. 1975.

The National Economic and Development Authority. (Brochure). Manila. 1976.

Sri Lanka Association for the Advancement of Science. *Thirty-second Annual Session: Physical Planning and National Development.* Colombo, 1976.

United Nations. *Organization and Administration of Public Enterprises.* U.N. Publication. E.68.II.H.1.

United Nations. *ECE Symposium on problems relating to environment.* U.N. Publication. E.71.II.E.6.

United Nations. *Organization, Management and Supervision of Public Enterprises in Developing Countries.* U.N. Publication E.74.II.H.4.

United Nations. *Organization and Administration of Environmental Programmes.* U.N. Publication. E.74.II.H.5.

United Nations. *Development Administration: Current Approaches and Trends in Public Administration for National Development.* U.N. Publication. E.76.II.H.1.

CHAPTER 7

The "Total Environment" Idea

1. Holistic Relationships in Environmental Management

"Our co-operating governments have established departments to improve environmental situations," the international adviser lamented, "but most of the efforts have been shotgun attempts—the pellets have hit the targets everywhere and hurt them nowhere."

The natural tendency is to divide areas of work so that specialized technology can be applied to each set of similar tasks. In environmental work at the policy, legislative and administrative levels this is also a natural predilection.

It is essential, however, to see the environment itself as one and indivisible. The challenge is to approach the environment as a whole area for administration while still leaving open the options for dividing technological tasks among expert groups. If the environment itself is "divided up" in administrative thinking there will emerge automatically a fragmented and sporadic attack upon environmental problems. The real need is to tackle problems as parts of an interconnected whole. Co-ordination is the essence of effectiveness but it is possibly the most difficult of all administrative tasks.

To achieve an holistic relationship in environmental management the primary elements are:

a. a policy for the environment applying to all governmental levels—national, regional and local;

b. legislation and regulation at all levels of government which binds government agencies, the private sector, the community at large; and *c.* an integrated and co-ordinated administration at all levels of government, working in co-operation with the private sector and all citizens.

Elaboration of these ideas is contained in Chaps. 6, 9 and 14. The traditional bureaucratic passion for isolating responsibilities and assigning administrative units to serve them must be viewed with scepticism in this whole environmental field. If the wholeness of the environment is not appreciated, there can be no efficient administration along conventional lines.

2. Comprehensive Attack on Environmental Problems

Various approaches to environmental challenges as outlined in Chap. 6 all have shortcomings. The need is to develop a national strategy at the highest governmental levels and to implement programmes by a co-ordinated decentralized effort spread throughout all levels of government and the community. In this regard it is essential for a comprehensive attack on environmental problems to incorporate the following factors:

a. establishing a national "total environment" policy:
b. strengthening the powers and widening the responsibilities of existing single-mission governmental agencies to enable them to take more effective actions to manage the environment;
c. integrating the elements within this traditional method through a completely new approach with an inter-agency body co-ordinating the environmentally oriented activities of the single-mission authorities;
d. binding the private sector into the national environment through the decision-making role of government agencies at all levels;
e. bringing the best available minds to bear on the broad problems of the "total environment" through a scientific and technological consultative council, comprising environmental officials, academics, consultants and industrialists;

f. establishing an environmental management system to foster continuous dialogue on environmental matters and to inject the environmental dimension into national, regional and local levels of government and throughout the private sector;

g. involving the whole community in a national environmental enhancement campaign through a comprehensive training, education and communication campaign, and

h. establishing a high-level national environment council to elaborate and review continuously broadly based national environmental strategies binding on government agencies, the private sector and the whole community, and to provide effective environmental input to national economic and social development planning.

So much for the theory designed to bring the unity of the environment into harmony with the unity needed to manage it. The applied approach to the theory follows in the next chapters.

Selected Bibliography

Beale, J. G., Minister for Environmental Control, Government of New South Wales. *Improvement of the Environment: Management of Pollution.* Government Printer, Sydney, Australia. 1971.

Beale, J. G., Minister for Environmental Control, Government of New South Wales. *Guidelines for Application of Environmental Impact Policy in New South Wales.* Government Printer, Sydney, Australia. 1973.

Beale, J. G., Minister for Environment Control, Government of New South Wales. *The Capsule of Environmental Progress in New South Wales.* Government Printer, Sydney, Australia. 1973.

Beale, J. G., *Draft Guide to Environment Protection and Management: A Basic for National Environmental Initiatives.* Prepared for discussion with the United Nations Environment Programme. UNEP, Nairobi, Kenya. 1975.

Suriyakumaran, C. *Environment Management Framework—Background Note.* (Informal paper). Regional Office for Asia and the Pacific, United Nations Environment Programme, Bangkok, Thailand. 1975.

Sachs, Ignacy. *Eco-development.* Ecole des Hautes Etudes, Paris. 1973.

CHAPTER 8

Investigating Environmental Management Initiatives

"How do you get such quick results from your national environmental management consultancies?" Although the preparatory work is arduous, the actual visits have been brief—usually a month. Results start flowing during the mission. The *modus operandi* seems straightforward. It is outlined below to help others.

Before going into detail it is sobering to ask the question: Why a *foreign* consultant? A foreign expert can be handicapped by his lack of knowledge of the particular values of the people in, and the special conditions of, a developing country. Often there are already specialists within the developing country itself who have adequate qualifications and experience. They could be of greater value to their own country if they could be withdrawn from routine tasks to concentrate on a special international aid project, perhaps receiving special training in working with foreign experts employed in their country.

It is just as easy for local experts to report at the end of the project to the international agency. Usually the cost will be less due to savings on expenses and due to the immediate access to members of his own community that a well-informed local expert has.

The proverbs of many nations convey the view that "prophets are without honour in their own land" and perforce foreign prophets achieve an aura of their own. The personal philosophy implicit in what follows is that local prophets, especially in quantity, are valuable people.

1. Data Gathering

a. The professional method is to enter a client country as adequately briefed as possible. A reasonable knowledge of its physical, climatic and geographical features; history, culture and development; and policy, law, administration and technology is essential.

b. As preparation, with the prime objective of making the best use of time available in the client country, key information areas needing amplification for the expeditious conduct of the assignment are listed as follows:

(i) *Key Individual and Group Discussions*
- Appropriate members of national Cabinet
- Responsible ranking officials of government
- Responsible city administrators
- Leaders in science, technology and conservation
- Leaders in socio-economic fields
- Leaders in business, commerce, industry
- Other individuals and organizations deemed appropriate and important by the Government
- Suggestions for meetings with combinations of individuals, departmental representatives and organizations considered more helpful as groups than as individual contacts

(ii) *Basic Data*
- Relevant legislation, decrees, official reports and documents, technical papers, research studies, influential and responsible press articles referring to contamination of air and water, noise pollution, conservation of nature, national parks and wildlife, recreation, quality of urban and rural life, demography, extension work
- Preliminary listing of appropriate environmental legislation and its administration showing areas of jurisdiction and official procedures
- Government organization charts

(iii) *Field Inspections*
Prior to arrival the client government is asked for its suggestions for field inspections with special reference to:
- Air pollution

- Water pollution
- Noise pollution
- Waste disposal (municipal and industrial)
- Conservation projects (soil, water, forest, fishery, mining, wildlife)
- City planning—theory and practice
- Regional planning—theory and practice
- Project planning development
- Other areas the client considers important

c. On arrival a briefing session with senior governmental officials is held. Usually, this tests the adequacy of consultancy preparation and leads to new sources of information.

d. Discussions are held with a wide spectrum of people, including members of the political arm of government, officials of the executive arm, city and local government administrators; leaders in law, science, technology and socio-economic fields, leaders in agriculture, industry and commerce, members of various private organizations and a variety of individuals. These interviews indicate the level of environmental knowledge and concern in government, the private sector and the community at large. Further, they provide recognition of how well policies are working and give an impression of future needs. During this cross-sectional sampling diverse attitudes, areas of dissent and antagonism, toughness-of-mind towards financial sacrifice and so on, begin to surface.

e. Local references are perused. These include the national constitution, statutes, official documents and reports, maps, plans, photographs, press articles, technical publications and research studies. This increases understanding of the national position and further knowledge of the actual environmental situation.

f. A preliminary survey is made of the existing law covering pollution control, management of natural resources and environmental planning. This indicates the degree of fragmentation and the force of the law. There is emphasis on discovering whether a scattering of legal measures has caused any confusion among government agencies, the private sector and the community generally. Further information is sought as to whether fragmentation has reduced the effectiveness of current legal measures for mounting an adequate attack

on environmental problems. There is a search also for evidence
of legal instruments which are virtually inoperative, unenforced, or
unenforceable.

g. Simultaneously, a survey is made of the governmental administrative structure involved in environmental activities. This gives an
idea of omissions and redundancies. Further, evidence is sought
on "single mission" environmental management by individual agencies, operating within their own statutory charters. The corollary
is of course to seek out attempts (however abortive) to achieve
overall supervision, information, interchange, integration and co-
ordination of management decisions.

h. Coincident with these activities, environmental expertise and
experience available in government agencies is identified and the
level of this knowledge assessed. Also, the extent to which the specialized agencies, the private sector and the community are aware of,
and using this existing knowledge, is examined.

i. Specific field inspections organized by the client government
are made. These provide background information on environmental
achievements and also on environmental deterioration and expose
the reasons for the latter. Where successes are being achieved, the
fact also becomes obvious but, paradoxically, the reasons for success
are not always as obvious as those for failure.

j Academic institutions and research centres are visited, first to
assess the standard of competence of people engaged in environmentally-oriented activities. More important, one discovers very promptly
how effectively they relate to challenges originating outside Academe.

k. The talents and enthusiasm of those working, and those who
have the potential to work, in environmental management are
assessed. Their leadership qualities and potential for working success-
fully in multi-disciplinary and multi-agency operations are examined.

l. Training, education and communication services are discussed
with institutions, officials, groups, teachers, students and members
of the public. It is important to judge effectiveness, especially at
the grass roots level.

m. Discussions with industry leaders and business organizations
and groups to assess attitudes and policies towards environmental
management and pollution control measures.

2. Report Preparation

Time is expended most generously in prior preparation and on-the-spot basic data gathering. From here on it is possible to look realistically at the opportunities for comprehensive environmental management. Pollution control, management of natural resources and environmental planning are the areas of concern. The elements needed will be initiatives to achieve the indicated national goal—usually a practically possible improvement in the quality of life. The primary information is then treated as follows:

- Ideas are tested progressively. They are floated at meetings with representatives of government agencies and other appropriate agencies and personnel. The aim is to devise solutions which are practicable in the local scene.
- A preliminary report is prepared and discussed in draft form at further meetings with representatives of governmental agencies and other relevant personnel.
- The final report is completed promptly. It includes firm recommendations and also, most important, an action plan to implement these.

Following most of my professional consultancies extending over a period of 33 years, taking in some sixty countries, in all continents, my clients have confirmed that my efforts on their behalf have been successful. It is of course difficult to measure the success of one's own endeavours, especially in some environmental fields where often only time will tell. Believing my methods work I will proceed in the next chapter to examine the environmental administration process by my usual approach.

Selected Bibliography

Beale, J. G. *Protection and Management of the Thailand Environment. Phase I. Policy, Legislative and Administrative Initiatives.* Prepared for the United Nations Environment Programme at the request of the Government of Thailand. National Environment Board, Bangkok, Thailand. 1974.

Beale, J. G. *Management of the Venezuelan Environment. Phase I: Policy, Legislative and Administrative Initiatives.* Prepared for the United Nations Environment Programme at the request of the Government of the Republic of Venezuela. Venezuelan National Council on Environment, Caracas, Venezuela. 1975.

Beale, J. G. *Improvement of the Thailand National Environment Administration and Some Other Related Matters.* National Environment Board, Bangkok, Thailand. 1976.

Beale, J. G. *Environmental Management in the Philippines. Phase I: Policy, Legal and Administrative Initiatives.* Prepared for the Regional Office for Asia and the Pacific, United Nations Environment Programme, at the request of the Government of the Republic of the Philippines. Office of the President, Metro Manila, The Philippines. 1977.

Beale, J. G. *Environment Management in Sri Lanka. Phase I: Policy, Legislative and Administrative Initiatives.* Prepared for the Regional Office for Asia and the Pacific, United Nations Environment Programme at the request of the Government of Sri Lanka. Office of the Prime Minister, Colombo, Sri Lanka. 1977.

CHAPTER 9

Environmental Administration as a Process

1. Inter-related Activities

"We have many environmental projects", the bureaucrat said, then admitted, "The general position, however, is no better." It isn't. Mostly it is worse, and can be seen to be so.

One of the simplest truths about environmental administration is that it is a process—a system. The system may look disjointed, because it usually is! In the next few pages the process is set out with some comment so that any competent administrator, manager or other interested participant can see where he is oriented relative to the functional units. He can also see why his particular interest is sometimes at a dead end. With all the skills at his command he will not succeed in making things happen unless he understands that a systems approach is fundamental to success.

Environmental administrative systems have one particular system-characteristic which is that subsystems below the level at which governments elect to enter the system become mandatory for success—superior subsystems are elective. Thus individual isolated "environment projects", common in most countries, are rarely tied into an environmental management process. Consequently they are funded sporadically in a scheme of shifting priorities for finance, unless the government has elected to move into environmental operations at a planning level. If that has happened, "environment projects" usually become part of an "environment programme" with regular sustaining resources available.

The environmentally oriented activities of a country can be reviewed against the background of an environmental management process. One possible view of the inter-relationship is shown schematically in Fig. 7. The various functionary units and mechanisms can be seen as a system of co-ordinated activities.

The diagram shows how the hierarchy works out in its broadest units. An experienced bureaucrat can soon fit locally manufactured subunits into the slots if their names seem unfamiliar. The hierarchy is now reviewed, going from the upper to the lower levels.

2. International Environment Interest

Most governments have shown an International Environment Interest (*a*). For many governments this has been initially through their attendance at international and regional conferences, for example, the 1972 United Nations Conference on the Human Environment. This has led their environmental administration into co-operating with those in other countries at political, departmental, and sometimes economic levels.

In many cases the next step has been to become signatories to various international conventions, treaties, agreements and programmes dealing with environmental problems which spill over national boundaries, for example, the 1973 Convention on the Prevention of Marine Pollution by Dumping Wastes and Other Matters.

In the future, nations will almost certainly need to be even more concerned in international environmental activities, such as:

a. Acquisition of internationally available data and experience, supplemented by their own contributions to these pools of knowledge. For example, Earthwatch has four functions: evaluation, research, monitoring and information exchange. A Global Environmental Monitoring Systems (GEMS), an International Referral System (IRS) and an International Register of Potentially Toxic Chemicals (IRPTC) have been set up.

b. Determination of agreements on global standards, such as those dealing with disposal of dangerous wastes.

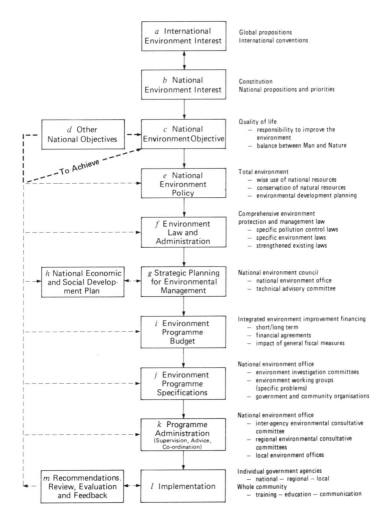

Fig. 7. Some Inter-related Activities of an Environmental Administration Process (*elaborated from Beale 1974*).

c. Adoption of regional standards and methods of procedure where they share resources with one or more other nations.
d. Enforcement of internationally agreed standards and procedures.

Nations which accept international obligations automatically activate national environmental management systems to implement those obligations. They also face the task of fitting agreed international propositions into national priorities for the environment.

3. National Environment Interest

Within the total world scene, nations face varying environmental challenges and therefore need to develop national propositions, priorities and responses suitable to their own circumstances.

Every country has a number of purely national interests: defence, food and development. The National Environment Interest (*b*) should take account of these associated national propositions and priorities. Conversely, other areas of national interest should include an environmental dimension. A common area where environmental issues always need consideration is in general employment policy.

It is essential for governments to establish a mechanism to provide environmental input at the highest level during the preparation of national plans and the implementation of resulting programmes.

4. National Environment Objective

Following consideration of international and national interest, an achievable environment objective needs to be formulated. It should be founded on a drive for improved quality of life based on accepting this governmental responsibility to its citizens. Conservation concepts related to wise use of natural resources are also essential foundations.

The National Environment Objective (*c*) is rarely expressed in precise terms. Sometimes it is indicated in the constitution and in a variety of declarations, pronouncements, decrees, as noted earlier.

The general environmental objective of most nations vaguely translates in practical management terms as the desire to enhance the environment through improvement programmes, while maintaining a balance between the activities of Man and the preservation of Nature.

To be viable an environmental objective must obviously be aligned with Other Objectives (*d*), such as defence, economic growth, energy policy, industrialization, income redistribution, social improvement. Presently, environmental objectives in many countries are *ad hoc* in nature. Usually they cannot be distinguished as inter-related components of total national objectives.

Governments need to take a closer look at their major national areas of policy to ensure there is appropriate relationship between them and that they include an environmental dimension which does not overshadow other objectives, but supplements them.

5. National Environment Policy

A National Environment Policy (*e*) should emphasize the necessity for wise use of total national resources (including people), with special stress on the conservation (wise use) of natural resources, to achieve a higher quality environment.

As has been noted, most countries have fragmented policies on a wide range of interests. There is little clear-cut expression of policy on pollution control, management of natural resources and environmental planning. This tends to confuse government agencies, the private sector and individuals.

The 1972 UNCHE Declaration (Part I) provides a useful basis for formulating national environmental policies. A nation needs to emphasize its own propositions and priorities concerning its environment in broad but readily comprehensible terms. Obviously it will wish to communicate orders of preference to citizens in a mode consistent with national traditions and values.

An environmental policy must be seen as essentially one component in overall national development planning. Obviously everything cannot be achieved at once so that it is important to devise a realistic policy.

Environmental policies can be formulated in several ways, for example, by the central governing body of the nation and adopted by the next echelons of regional or local government or by those echelons which can constitutionally promulgate actions under the aegis of national-level policies.

National environmental policies can be formulated as a short statement covering such aspects as:

- Ultimate balance between Man and Nature
- Maintenance of heritage, cultural and conservation values
- Essentiality of a quality environment
- Indication of the means of achieving quality
- Responsibilities of individual citizens, the private sector and all levels of government to contribute to improving the environment

The general announcement of environment policy priorities needs to be followed by a more detailed exposition of principles upon which the policy is founded. There also should be an indication of the detailed mechanisms by which the national policy will flow through the administration.

6. Environmental Law and Administration

To give effect to a national environment policy there is need for Environment Law and Administration (*f*), that is, law and administration which is ecologically oriented and both multi-disciplinary and multi-agency in approach. In most countries embarking on environmental management, it is necessary to review existing legislation and current administration, and to consider new initiatives in these areas. Formats for preliminary surveys of law and administration are included as Appendix I. Surveys of this kind were made in Thailand, Venezuela, Sri Lanka and the Philippines. In both Australia and New Zealand similar surveys were extended into useful guides to local environmental law.

A preliminary survey of national law and administration usually shows that the environment has already been regulated in part by existing laws. Mostly, these laws are administered by numerous "single-mission" agencies, such as administrations concerned specifically with soil, water, forests preservation, conservation, agricultural practices, health, hygiene, municipal waste, or transportation as illustrated in Fig. 8. The well-being of Man can undoubtedly be enhanced through the co-ordination of environmentally oriented approaches of individual agencies national, regional and local. Environmental deterioration is sometimes the result of either the law going unheeded by trespassers or failure on the part of individual agencies to administer their responsibilities effectively.

Surveys invariably reveal a fragmented approach to environmental law, indicating both overlapping and gaps. Also, when account is taken of regional and local laws, the need for new comprehensive environment management laws is obvious. Further, there is need for specific laws and regulations at all levels, covering such fields as noise abatement, waste disposal and environmental planning. There is usually need to amend, strengthen and/or extend the scope of some existing laws, and/or to relate them more specifically to environmental objectives, co-ordinated at all government levels to avoid confusion and promote co-operation between administering agencies. Arising from review there could be need for legislation such as:

- Organic law or enabling law to consolidate or set up comprehensive legislative controls
- Specific laws and regulations
- Amendment to existing laws to strengthen them, extend their scope, or relate them more specifically to environmental objectives

The response to the need to have consolidated environmental laws is usually disappointing. Reactions can be inept attempts to graft the laws of others (often the U.S.A. and U.K.) onto unsuitable local vehicles. Some also react by expecting that a single law, virtually manufactured by a computer will solve all problems.

Present administrative mechanisms to give effect to environmental law mirror its divisions, overlapping and deficiencies. This situation is reproduced at all governmental levels. Obviously, there is need for new and effectively administrative initiatives relating to:

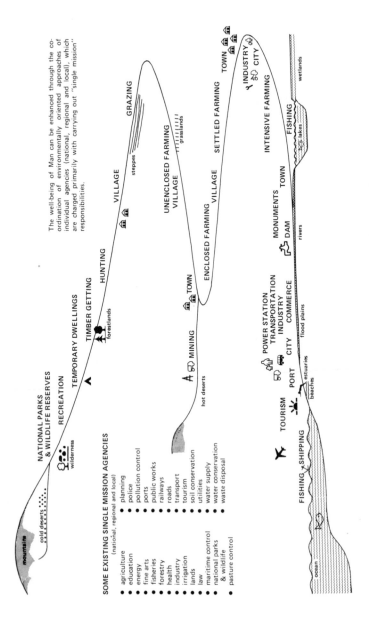

SOME EXISTING SINGLE MISSION AGENCIES
(national, regional and local)

- agriculture
- education
- energy
- fine arts
- fisheries
- forestry
- health
- industry
- irrigation
- lands
- law
- maritime control
- national parks & wildlife
- pasture control

- planning
- police
- pollution control
- ports
- public works
- railways
- roads
- transport
- tourism
- soil conservation
- utilities
- water supply
- water conservation
- waste disposal

The well-being of Man can be enhanced through the co-ordination of environmentally oriented approaches of individual agencies (national, regional and local), which are charged primarily with carrying out "single mission" responsibilities.

Fig. 8. Enhancing the Environment Through Co-ordinated Administration
(elaborated from Beale 1975)

- Mechanisms to co-ordinate national plans and programmes
- Financial arrangements and agreements to support administrative structures
- Structures to regionalize environmental management administration
- Control at regional and local government levels
- Enforcement of environmental laws at all levels

As the next step, it would be useful to list the environmental areas of responsibility under existing laws against the administering governmental agencies. A format for this purpose is included as Appendix II.

It would also be valuable to identify the expertise available in existing governmental agencies. A format for tabulating agencies against the characteristics and conditions of the environment is included as Appendix III.

7. Strategic Planning for Environmental Management

Environment policy in many countries is made up of several components with some essential elements such as land-use planning missing. Generally, there is governmental recognition that Strategic Planning for Environmental Management (g) and related programmes are needed to translate general national objectives into more definitive actions, but a way to achieve this has not yet been devised. Any action should of course be cognizant of spatial implications, targets (*e.g.* employment rates, population growth, pollution levels) and target dates, with emphasis on intermediate timing. Strategic planning should be reasonably detailed. Precision and accuracy can be progressively increased with experience. Points to consider are:

(i) Environment
  - Maintain heritage, cultural and conservation values, for example, historic monuments, seascape, landscape, wildlife

- Reach specific goals in the management of resources, for example, minerals, marine, agricultural, fishing, fossil fuels
- Reduce air, water, noise, visual and land pollution to specific levels

(ii) Human Well-being
- Improve human settlement quality to specific levels
- Identify disadvantaged groups and determine causes creating this, specifying remedial action

(iii) Efficiency
- Undertake studies of land capability systems
- Prepare specific purpose programmes, for example, land acquisition, services, transportation, health, housing, education, recreation, tourism, agriculture
- Prepare specific finance budgets to achieve targets

(iv) Equity
- Commence a full-scale public environmental education campaign
- Increase public involvement in planning processes
- Increase access of people to goods and services

(v) Flexibility
- Introduce environmental development planning at national, regional and local government levels and throughout the private sector
- Evaluate and review plans and programmes periodically
- Shift financial support to meet changing needs

(vi) Information
- Identify the current physical, biological and socio-economic characteristics of the total environment
- Assess current likely future trends in environmental degradation and/or enhancement
- Accelerate collection, collation and evaluation of information on natural and cultural environments
- Improve environmental training, education and information
- Promote environmental research and technology assessment

(vii) Law and Administration
  • Survey existing law and administration
  • Determine new law and administration necessary to support effectively the plan and programmes

At this level also the content of the national environment strategy should provide valuable input to the National Economic and Social Development Plan (*h*). As mentioned earlier a step in this direction is seen in The Fourth Five-Year Plan (1977–1981) of Thailand. As noted above, most present economic and social development plans lack an adequate environmental dimension.

8. Environment Programme Budget

Finance is a scarce resource and obviously must be allocated carefully in order to achieve national, regional and local objectives. If anything substantive is to happen, consideration must be given to an Environment Programme Budget (*i*). All governmental proposals compete for available finance and, increasingly, to achieve the ultimate delivery of services to citizens in line with their political objectives, governments need to be fully aware of both direct and indirect implications of expenditure.

In many developing countries there are corporate plans and budgets to assist governments to determine required levels and types of public investment. In order to fulfil currently developing national aspirations and citizen's needs, the allocation and uses should be brought into mesh with environmental planning objectives, which are to:

a. ensure efficient, equitable and socially desirable allocation of government finance; and
b. provide an appropriate climate for both governmental and private investment in development, with emphasis on the quality of life.

An environmental management plan cannot be realized unless it is supported by adequate finance. Governments have been investing for many years in projects such as purifying water supplies, sewage treatment and public hygiene. To forestall further environmental degradation, it is obvious that the investment will have to be increased in these and other environmental improvement areas.

Various governmental agencies (and some areas of the private sector) will doubtless be inclined to view their own sectoral programmes as being most significant. There is need therefore to point to the wisdom of introducing both short and long term priorities into an integrated system of environmental financing. To obtain the best results from the budget, this should take proper account of competing financial commitments, or other fiscal measures, designed to achieve other national objectives.

There may be need to provide environmentally oriented fiscal incentives to industries (and municipalities) to encourage them to provide additional anti-pollution measures. Similar incentives to farmers would encourage them to undertake measures to improve their local environment and thereby contribute to the enhancement of the total environment, for example, by tree-planting or by undertaking soil conservation.

9. Environment Programme Specifications

Most programmes are still implemented on technical and economic specifications. There is need to develop Environment Programme Specifications (j) which will give programmes an environmental orientation. This could probably be assisted by input from environmental investigation committees, working groups (on specific problems), governmental agencies and community organizations.

Examples of the injection of an environmental emphasis into a programme for the construction of a water storage system would be the funding of soil conservation measures on the catchment area to reduce siltation or measures to prevent the spreading of disease. Environmental constraints should be applied in planning an agricultural programme for a developing country. These obviously are different from those which should be applied where a second airport is to be provided near a big city in a developed country.

10. Programme Administration

Some administrations have already recognized the need to establish new institutional arrangements in order to translate national environment strategies, at all governmental levels, into sensible practical systems for detailed Programme Administration (*k*).

A new environmentally oriented administration will need to provide functions of supervision, advice, co-ordination and review. These are needed to ensure that the implementation of the programme is effective at national, regional and local levels, and will actively involve the private sector including individual citizens. This will require provision for additional technical, professional and managerial inputs.

In designing a new administration it is useful to consider environmental management linkages for which a possible synthesis is shown in Fig. 9. In doing this, consideration should also be given to the comments in Chaps. 10, 11 and 12.

The growing size and complexity of government often leads to over-centralization, inefficiency and poor performance. The centre of government can only really devote itself to the vital duties of supervision and control, and concentrate adequately on the most crucial problems if it is willing to delegate sufficient authority to individual units so as to allow them to function autonomously in the management of their respective operations. Control is centralized, execution is decentralized. The lower echelons must of course operate within the national guidelines.

11. Implementation

It can be seen that Implementation (*l*) is an all-pervasive function. Environmental administration, in common with the administration of finance and the administration of energy policy, calls for co-ordinated action across every area of governmental activity. It calls, even more so than do finance and energy, for action at the community level. As indicated in the previous chapter, some natural ordering

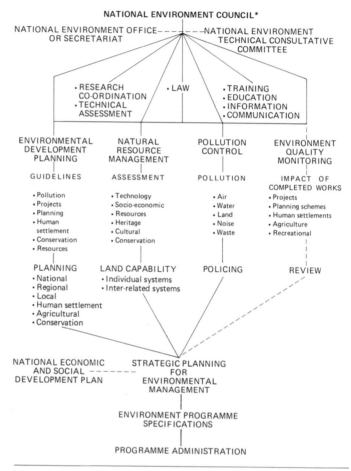

Fig. 9. Some Environmental Management Linkages—one possible synthesis
(*elaborated from Beale 1975*).

within three basic categories of administration, namely *pollution control, management of natural resources,* and *environmental planning* can be used to structure implementation within each tier of government.

Staff training and education is essential. See Chap. 13. All too frequently an educated elite, with no practical work experience, take control of the higher environmental policy functions (*e, f, g*). Usually the result is to starve the management echelons (*j, k, l*) of much needed skills, at the same time superimposing impractical goals on the whole system. Lack of work-tested policy people is a guaranteed recipe for administrative ineffectiveness—there is no substitute for a professional "apprenticeship". A top environmental administrator simply has to have experienced situations like an angry community bearing down on the smallest, most isolated office in his system if he is to understand how to respond at the highest policy level to "real life" problems.

12. Review, Evaluation and Feedback

More so than with other areas of administration, environmental work depends on reacting surely and precisely to changing community perceptions and values. Review, Evaluation and Feedback (*m*) to every functional administrative level is therefore particularly important. If policies, programmes and plans are not evaluated continuously and the results relayed promptly to the appropriate administrative area, there can only be one outcome—a monolithic fossilization of attitudes. In practical terms, the government will quickly realize that it is making the wrong responses to the right issues and it will not be easy for it, in the absence of established feedback procedures, to pinpoint what has gone wrong. Policy areas will be particularly vulnerable if their administrators are not practical people, used to adjusting to changed circumstances.

13.

Implementation (*l*) and Review, Evaluation and Feedback (*m*) together complete the national part of the environmental administration cycle illustrated in Fig. 7. It is important to note that the various parts of the process only work when the relevant cycles are "closed". For example, the National Environment Objective (*c*) cannot be achieved unless this part of the cycle is closed. Also Other National Objectives (*d*) can be co-ordinated or activated by the "recycling" of environmental programmes through them.

Selected Bibliography

Conferences

United Nations Conference on the Human Environment. Stockholm, Sweden. 2–16 June 1972.
United Nations Law of the Sea Conference (continuing).
United Nations Conference on Human Settlements (HABITAT). Vancouver, Canada. 30 May to 11 June 1976.
United Nations Conference on Desertifications (UNCOD). Nairobi, Kenya. 29 August to 9 September.

Declarations

Declaration on the Establishment of a New International Economic Order (NIEO). 1974.
Charter of Economic Rights and Duties of States. 1974.
Cocoyoc Declaration. 1974.
Lima Declaration and Plan of Action on Industrial Development and Co-operation. 1974.

Conventions

International Convention for the Regulation of Whaling. 1948.
Convention on the Continental Shelf. 1964.
International Convention for the Prevention of the Pollution of the Sea by Oil. 1954, 1962, 1973.
The Convention on the Prevention of Marine Pollution by Dumping of Wastes and Other Matters. 1973.

Treaties

Banning Nuclear Tests in the Atmosphere, in Outer Space and Under Water. 1963.
The Antarctic Treaty. 1961.

Agreements

Agreement between Government of Australia and Government of Japan for the Protection of Migratory Birds and Birds in Danger of Extinction and their Environment. 1974.
Plant Protection Agreement for the South East Asian and Pacific Region. 1976.

Programmes

United Nations Environment Programme (UNEP).
Integrated Global Ocean Station System
Global Environmental Monitoring System (GEMS).
International Referral System (IRS).
International Register of Potentially Toxic Chemicals (IRPTC).

CHAPTER 10

Pollution Control

1. Pollution Control Approach

"That's not pollution, it's industrial progress", said the bureaucrat gazing proudly at the factory chimneys belching smoke in an industrial city of a developing country. It is having its industrial revolution. Officials echo the sentiments of earlier industrialists and economists of developed countries, "Where there's smoke, there are jobs". Even today in some developing and developed countries civic leaders join industrialists in actions to delay upgrading effluent treatment systems on the grounds that the cost would have a disastrous effect on the local economy. It would "kill the goose that lays the golden egg". There are of course costs to consider, including the cost to the environment. Citizens frequently say, "Everything has become dirtier, but I suppose it's the price you pay for progress." Often pollution has been the price. But this need not necessarily be so.

Pollution control relates to measures to minimize air, water, land, noise, visual and other pollution, and the disposal of solid and liquid waste. Pollution in many forms has always attended human activities. It has intensified under increased population pressures. Industrial pollution has added a further order of magnitude. The load on the environment has been extended by modern transportation and tourism. In most countries there are examples where pollution has already accelerated beyond the capacity of many local environments to absorb the residuals of a mass consumption society.

Environmental degradation problems vary from country to country, but there are some well defined differences between the

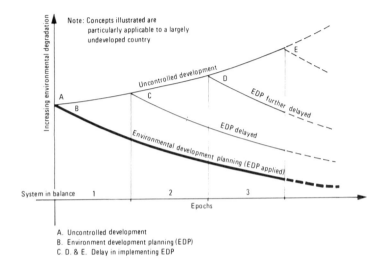

A. Uncontrolled development
B. Environment development planning (EDP)
C. D. & E. Delay in implementing EDP

Fig. 10. Effect of Delaying Environmental Development Planning (*elaborated from Beale 1975*).

situations in developing and developed countries. Diagrammatically, Fig. 10, generally applicable to a largely undeveloped country where pollution is small, shows the possible adverse environmental effect. This results primarily from the accelerating rate of destruction of natural resources, consequent upon delaying the implementation of environmental development planning.

Historically, regulatory attacks on environmental degradation in developed countries can be considered as occurring in three epochs—the environmental past emphasizing pollution control and simple development control; the present emphasizing natural resources management; and the future which will look to environmental development planning, as shown in Fig. 11. By taking account of water contamination and health problems this illustration can be applied equally to developing countries.

Pollution control is a primary consideration in environmental management programmes and has an important role to play in checking environmental degradation. It tends to be a backward-

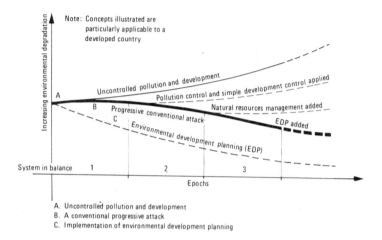

A. Uncontrolled pollution and development
B. A conventional progressive attack
C. Implementation of environmental development planning

Fig. 11. Effect of a Conventional Progressive Attack on Environmental
Degradation (*elaborated from Beale 1975*).

looking operation at first. It concentrates on remedying the results
of poor planning, poor or obsolescent technology, and/or backward
attitudes to the environment. For the future it takes a fairly short-term
approach. Medium-term approaches take over as soon as pollution
control increases and the emphasis shifts to natural resources management (Refer to Chap. 11). The next shift is to environmental development planning approaches which provide more effective medium-
and long-term safeguards against pollution (Refer to Chap. 12).

As set out below, a short-term approach to environmental management through pollution control can be considered in graded steps.
Steps do not have to follow each other automatically. There could
possibly be simultaneous applications. Very often, however, pragmatism dictates a sequence of pollution control systems running from
"best available means", to "source standards", to "ambient standards", to "pollution charges" or other "economic incentives".
Strategies to effect these controls range from simple monetary penalties, to the generalized "polluter pays" principle and on to fairly
sophisticated economic approaches. A well-aimed programme is
essential if steady progress is to be achieved.

2. *Pollution Control Techniques*

While none of the approaches (*a*) to (*e*) below is a cure-all, in practice these various devices will be used eventually, and they can all assist in reducing pollution. Their individual shortcomings should not be allowed to obscure the fact that the implementation of a comprehensive range of pollution controls with a balanced combination of engineering, education and enforcement, can effectively reduce environmental degradation from pollution.

a. Best Available Means

The objective of this technique is to see that industries, municipalities and other polluters (government and private) apply the best technology available to them in their situation. The approach is relatively easy to implement by legislation and, because of the pragmatism inherent in it, is flexible in administration. Inspection is not a difficult task even with only moderately skilled inspectors. The drawback is that pollution tends to be brought under control slowly and also tends to improve only to a particular point. Industry is not forced to improve its position in absolute terms—the whole concept is applied relative to yesterday's technology. Nevertheless, in some developing situations this control method can be the best starting point.

b. Source Standards

A logical extension of "best available means" is to superimpose emission standards on sources. Legislatively, this is not difficult, but the standards to be used need to be determined realistically. In turn, this presupposes that local scientific and technological skills are sufficient to set standards and to measure pollutant emissions when control is exercised over pollution sources. The approach tends to be piecemeal unless there is a clearly expressed and executed desire on the part of governments to impose penalties consistently.

c. Ambient Standards

A more complex elaboration of emission sources control is to set ambient standards, which specify the level of pollution to which a pollutant may be permitted to raise the local level on discharge. These are referenced regionally and relate to standards which need a great amount of skill and technology to determine. Air standards for such gases as ozone, sulphur dioxide, carbon monoxide are examples.

In this case, control moves from an individual (and therefore piecemeal) to an overall management control method. Overall management relies on a regional monitoring network to signal that the whole regional water, air, or waste disposal system is overloaded at particular locations.

d. Polluter Pays Principle

The approaches outlined above (best available means, source standards, ambient standards) are all technologically based. The "polluter pays" principle is an adjunct and is economically based, at least overtly.

It is sometimes difficult in practice to separate the polluters' payments from the community's payments. If polluters (*e.g.* industries or municipalities) are charged they tend to pass the payment on to the consuming public in higher prices or taxes. Fines and other sanctions to force the system to work are also often difficult to apply at a level which will ensure effectiveness.

Imposition of the "polluter pays" principle has a chance, however, of being counter-productive where the principle is implemented by governments essentially as a short-term avenue to revenue, thus avoiding central treasury expenditure on an overall environmental programme.

e. Economic Incentive Approaches

The other economic incentives which can be used relate to encouraging industries or entire human settlements to adopt improved anti-pollution measures out of sheer self-interest. Instead of arbitrary fines or other difficult-to-apply sanctions, the polluter is charged per unit of pollutant for whatever he allows to escape. This should not be seen as a licence to pollute because prosecution under the law is always possible.

The scale of charges can be applied on some very gross measure such as total BOD discharged in the case of water, set so that the polluter has the option of changing location if the charge is uneconomic to him, or improving the effluent discharges to an economic level, or eliminating them completely and avoiding all charges.

Schemes like this can be nationally economical. At first polluters for whom pollution control is cheap will implement control programmes. It is usually possible to remove the first portion of pollution at a low cost as indicated in Fig. 12. Accordingly, for a given national budget of pollution control funds there is relatively maximum environmental improvement. The system of charges can also be used as a tool for implementing regional development policy.

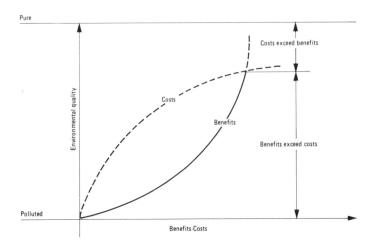

Fig. 12. Benefit–Cost Relationship for Pollution Control—schematic (*elaborated from Beale 1975*).

f. Some Other Points

With the advent of a comprehensive national environment strategy there will be need for individual government agencies to draw up specific pollution standards for use within their own areas of responsibility. It is important to recognize that these standards should be certified by the national environmental authority as being within the broad national guidelines and should be related specifically to each particular local environment. It would be useful in this regard to study potential pollution problems, and a format for a preliminary survey is included as Appendix IV.

It must be recognized that an environmental programme based solely on pollution control treats the symptoms of environmental degradation without curing the disease. The pollution control programme must therefore be co-ordinated with natural resources management and environmental planning programmes.

3. Immediate Actions

Increasing population, and with it improved standards of living, will create an urgent need to minimize the increasing incidence of pollution. While action is being considered or taken to establish a strong specialist antipollution organization it is desirable and usually possible to take immediately beneficial administrative actions. For example, the activities of medical officials spread throughout a developing country could include some pollution control duties. In rural areas their efforts could be strengthened by the provision of such things as simple water testing kits. The national pollution control effort could be immediately strengthened by an administrative order requiring those agencies concerned to enforce existing legislation within their jurisdictions.

Selected Bibliography

Air Pollution

Organization for Economic Co-operation and Development. *Policy Towards the Creation of Vehicle-Free Areas in Cities.* OECD, Paris. 1972.

Organization for Economic Co-operation and Development. *Emission Measurement Techniques for Particulate Matter from Power Plants, Cement Manufacture and the Iron and Steel Industry.* OECD, Paris. 1975.

Organization for Economic Co-operation and Development. *Report on the Use of Dose and Effects Data in Setting Air Quality Standards to Provide a Basis for the Control of Sulphur Oxides.* Experience in Germany, Japan and United States. OECD, Paris. 1975.

Organization for Economic Co-operation and Development. *Report on the Use of Techniques to Provide Air Quality Information for Land-Use Planning.* OECD, Paris. 1976.

Department of the Environment. *Chlorofluoro-Carbons and Their Effect on Stratospheric Ozone.* Pollution Paper No. 5. Her Majesty's Stationery Office, London. 1976.

Department of the Environment. *Effects of Airborne Sulphur Compounds on Forests and Freshwaters.* Pollution Paper No. 7. Her Majesty's Stationery Office, London. 1976.

Water Pollution

Food and Agricultural Organization (FAO) and World Health Organization (WHO). *Health Implications of Water-Related Parasitic Diseases in Water Development Schemes.* Geneva. 1967.

Water Resources Council. *Establishment of Principles and Standards of Planning—Water and Related Land Resources.* Federal Register, Vol. 38, No. 174, September 10, 1973.

Reynolds, Peter J. *Environmental Indicators in River Basin Management.* Proceedings of Tokyo Symposium, International Association for Scientific Hydrology. Tokyo, Japan. December, 1975.

Department of the Environment. *The Separation of Oil from Water for North Sea Oil Operations.* Pollution Paper No. 6. Her Majesty's Stationery Office, London. 1976.

Department of the Environment. *Accidental Oil Pollution of the Sea.* Pollution Paper No. 8. Her Majesty's Stationery Office, London. 1976.

Noise Pollution

Organization for Economic Co-operation and Development. *Charging for Noise.* OECD, Paris. 1976.

Organization for Economic Co-operation and Development. *Social Cost of Noise.* OECD, Paris, 1976.

Economics

Hardin, G. *The Tragedy of the Commons.* Science, 162, 1243–48, pp. 172–182. 1968.

Walker, William R. (Ed.). *Economics of Air and Water Pollution.* Water Resources Research Center. Virginia Polytechnic Institute, Balcksburg, Virginia, U.S.A. 1969.

Bohm, P. and Kneese, V. (Ed.). *The Economics of Environment*. Papers from Four Nations. 1971.

Kneese, A. V. and Schultze, C. L. *Pollution, Prices and Public Policy*. The Brookings Institution, Washington, D.C. 1975.

Johannesson, Margareta. *Dynamic Aspects of the Use of Prices for Protecting the Environment*. Swedish Journal of Economics. June 1972.

American Economic Journal. *Pollution Abatement Subsidies*. December, 1972.

Organization for Economic Co-operation and Development. *Environmental Damage Costs*. OECD, Paris. 1974.

Organization for Economic Co-operation and Development. *The Polluter Pays Principle: Definition, Analysis, Implementation*. OECD, Paris. 1975.

Organization for Economic Co-operation and Development. *Pollution Charges. An Assessment*. OECD, Paris. 1976.

Monitoring

International Engineering Service Consortium Pty. Ltd. *Feasibility study for an automatic pollution monitoring network for air, water and noise in the Sydney regional area (the first module of a national network)*. Prepared under the direction of the Minister for Environment Control, New South Wales, J. G. Beale. Sydney, Australia. 1973.

International Council of Scientific Unions Scientific Committee on Problems of the Environment. *Global Environmental Monitoring System (GEMS)*. SCOPE 3. SCOPE, Paris, 1973.

Department of the Environment. *The Monitoring of the Environment in the United Kingdom*. Pollution Paper No. 1. Her Majesty's Stationery Office, London. 1974.

PA Management Consultants Pty Limited. *Study of the technical and economic factors involved in the development of air monitoring networks in Australia*. Prepared for the Australian Environment Council, Canberra, Australia. 1974.

Organization for Economic Co-operation and Development. *Report on Use of Surveillance and Control Techniques for Air Pollution Alert Systems*. OECD, Paris. 1976.

General

Department of the Environment. *Lead in the Environment and Its Significance to Man*. Pollution Paper No. 2. Her Majesty's Stationery Office, London. 1974.

Department of the Environment. *The Non-Agricultural Uses of Pesticides in Great Britain*. Pollution Paper No. 3. Her Majesty's Stationery Office, London. 1974.

Lesaca, Reynaldo M. *Pollution Control Legislation and Experience in a Developing Country: The Philippines*. The Journal of Developing Areas. Vol. 8, No. 4. Western Illinois University, Illinois, U.S.A. 1974.

Department of the Environment. *Controlling Pollution.* Pollution Paper No. 4. Her Majesty's Stationery Office, London. 1975.

Holmes, Nicholas (Ed.). *Environment and the Industrial Society.* Hodder & Stoughton, London. 1976.

A Subcommittee in Collaboration with the National Science Council of Sri Lanka. *Environmental Management in Sri Lanka.* Report. Government Publications Bureau, Colombo, Sri Lanka. 1973 (published 1976).

National Science Council of Sri Lanka. *Man and his Environment.* Seminar, 9 March 1976. Colombo, Sri Lanka.

Economic Commission for Europe. *Steps Towards a System of Environmental Statistics.* Warsaw Conference, 15–19 October, 1973. Geneva. 1973.

CHAPTER 11

Management of Natural Resources

1. Approach to the Management of Natural Resources

"Forests dwindle, farm lands erode, deserts encroach, rivers silt, flooding increases, fisheries disappear", the concerned administrator said. "Our tree-planting campaigns, agricultural reforms, family planning and other programmes are not holding the line. We're headed for destitution." This is said, often by able people who appreciate the problems but whose efforts to overcome them are frustrated by misguided national priorities.

There is ample evidence everywhere, both visible and documentary, of the deterioration of terrestrial and marine resources. Lack of realistic corrective and preventative measures is also apparent. Oddly, there is usually enough existing local and international data available in the form of reports, maps, photographs and documents on natural resources to provide adequate informational input for the preparation of national environmental guidelines for the conservation (wise use) of resources. Due to either a lack of concern or of will, this essential work usually remains to be done. Often a number of solutions to pressing problems can flow from consideration of existing information, provided there are options available for the future. Any attack aimed at long-term solutions must necessarily be based on a sound scientific approach.

Resource management is usually concerned with optimum allocation of resources including land, natural features, capital and labour. In most countries increasing population, urbanization, commerce, industrialization, transportation and tourism have accelerated pressures for land development. This has imposed competing demands for the retention and use of land for purposes of preservation, conservation, agriculture, urban development, major projects, industry, mining, recreation and tourist facilities.

Most countries need to prepare a comprehensive national environment strategy in which the allocation and subsequent management of resources, particularly natural resources, are important components.

Effective pollution control can itself divert residual resources such as energy, municipal waste, industrial effluents, eroding soil, dirty water, and useless land to more valuable employment. Well-managed resources rarely contribute to significant pollution.

2. Environmental "Outer Limits"

The developments of mankind must avoid transgressing environmental "outer-limits", that is, those constraints imposed by the "biosphere". We know that the earth is finite in size and in the energy it receives from the sun, but we do not know accurately its "carrying capacity" for man and his activities. Therefore we must be ever vigilant to recognize significant signs which point to the likely destruction of any part of the biosphere, for example, the ozone layer.

There must also be awareness of "local outer-limits". Parts of the biosphere differ in "resilience", that is, in their resistance to natural changes and to various human impacts. It had been thought that diverse, dominant systems, for example, tropical forests, were fairly stable and that species-poor systems under the stress of harsh environments, like deserts were relatively fragile. Research now suggests a more complicated relationship between diversity and stability. For example, a large proportion of the essential nutrients in a tropical forest system is often within the trees. Should cutting and burning disperse these nutrients and bare the soil with resulting erosion, much of the fertility in the system may be quickly lost. Furthermore, it is known that temperate zones have areas where, despite continuous cultivation over long periods, robust soils have remained fertile. Such differences in the capacities of various systems to sustain biological productivity when used by Man can set appropriate "local outer-limits."

3. Ecosystem Management Concept

It is essential to have an integrated approach to the management of natural resources through a concept of "ecosystem management". This idea is shown schematically by Smith and Hill in Fig. 13, which gives a rough indication of the relationship of several managed ecosystems in terms of the degree of management and biological diversity. As urban areas are expanded, principally by the influx

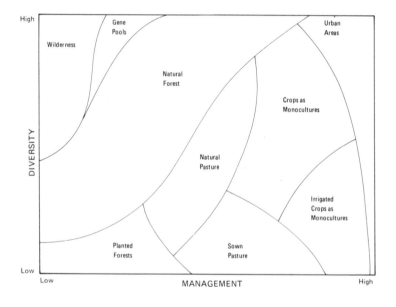

Fig. 13. The Relationship of Several Managed Ecosystems in Terms of Degree of Management and Biological Diversity (*Smith and Hill 1975*).

of impoverished rural populations, increasing demands for food, building materials and urban land, the response of agriculture has been to expand crops into natural pasture, convert forest into natural pasture, overcut natural forests and so on. Urban growth and consequent conservation awareness "squeezes" agriculture which can only meet the pressure by intensification of farming. This means more intensive use of fertilizer, insecticides or herbicides, higher energy inputs, and a resultant call for capital rather than labour.

Many of the environmentally degrading results of the dynamic inter-relationships traced above occur because the scientific and technological personnel involved have been "imprisoned" in strict disciplines and therefore fail to communicate adequately. In order to manage the natural resources segment effectively institutional arrangements have to ensure effective integration of these presently separated specialized skills.

4. Land Capability Approach

An effective means of achieving efficient resource allocation (land use) is by developing "land capability" systems which indicate basic constraints as well as opportunities in environmental planning. Land capability refers to the suitability, potential and intrinsic value of an area for particular or multiple uses.

Land capabilities are flexible concepts for environmental planning purposes. Plans which are based on land capability systems can indicate environmental capabilities—the extent to which development is compatible with environmental aims; the specific developmental exclusions which might be necessary; the environmental standards needed to preserve land capabilities.

Once land has been used it is generally difficult or impossible to restore it to its original state. Sometimes this can be due to lack of knowledge needed to reverse the use process, or it can be because restoration is too costly. Where recovery can be effected, it is usually only possible through high cost programmes needing co-ordinated multi-disciplinary research into the relationships between population, development, environment and resource management, followed by expensive "pilot plant" operations as a prelude to restoring both the resource and the confidence of people in its rehabilitation. Wise initial allocation of land therefore permits achievement of the best immediate and future use.

5. Cyclic Ecological Changes in a Land System

In order clearly to understand this dynamic equilibrium, it is useful to consider the cyclic ecological changes which a land system may undergo. A forest land system is shown schematically in Fig. 14.

Generally, in the forest example given, these changes may be described as:

(i)   original virgin forest ecosystems—plants, wildlife, wilderness;
(ii) modified—managed for timber, wildlife utilization, recreation, shifting agriculture, reserved wilderness (deliberate non-use);
(iii) transformed—replaced by forest plantations, mines, grazing, farming, settlements, roads, reservoirs, recreation, tourism;
(iv) degraded—erosion, desertification, invasion of weed species, salting, pollution.

Looked at from the viewpoint of the natural capital of the land these four stages can be described as:

(i)   capital intact—heritage, cultural value, genetic resource;
(ii) capital in forest—intact until timber and wildlife assets are realized;
(iii) capital in soil;
(iv) capital reduced or lost.

From a management cost viewpoint (to maintain dynamic equilibrium) the stages relate as follows:

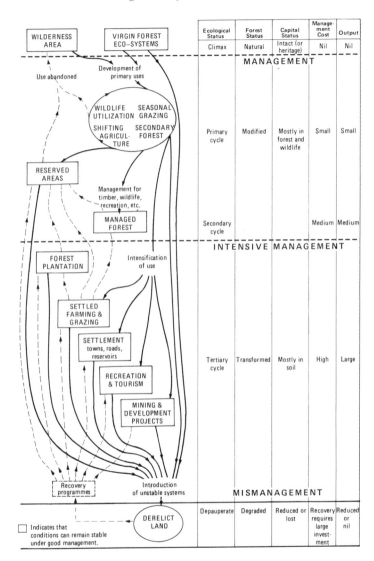

Fig. 14. Allocation of Forest Land for Possible Uses—an example of renewable resource management and consequences (*elaborated from Beale 1975*).

    (i)   no management costs;
    (ii) small to medium management costs;
    (iii) high management costs;
    (iv) recovery requires large investment (super costs).

Output of economic services flows as follows:

    (i)   nil;
    (ii) small to medium;
    (iii) large
    (iv) reduced, nil, or negative (economic resources are consumed).

It will be seen that unless land is allocated in accordance with its capabilities, the risk of environmental degradation is high and therefore a system to establish and review land use needs to be constructed on reliable bases. Generally, the further the departure in land use from the natural state the higher is the investment required in money and manpower to maintain the land in a desired state or to repair devastation when this occurs.

6. Water Resource Management

As a general rule, conceptualization of land systems as ecosystems can be achieved by considering water as the integrating element. Watersheds, defining the catchment areas, tend also to define physical units of land and therefore can be used as planning units.

Some care is needed to see that the physical convenience of the catchment area approach is not over-used or over-simplified.

Accordingly, this important subject is reviewed below.

Management of water for a variety of human uses tends to occur in a piecemeal manner without due attention to the integrity of the water cycle. "The world bank of water remains constant." Water intrinsically does not change in character although it becomes polluted, salinized, frozen and so on. When it flows as run-off in water courses, percolates through soils, is stored in aquifers, is diverted, or impounded in dams or reservoirs, is processed, treated for drinking, industrial, irrigation and recreation purposes, cleaned for use and re-use, it is ultimately returned to the world water bank, as shown in Figs. 15 and 16. In a sense it is not a renewable resource—it is very much a resource in the same class as land.

The augmentation of agricultural, industrial, municipal and other water supplies is generally planned as a single-purpose mission with scant regard for such river basin constraints as upstream plant cover and farming practices, or downstream soils and fisheries, or its influence on resources in adjoining valleys and oceans.

Water resources just as much as land resources need comprehensive, environmentally oriented basic studies to show clearly available options to policy and decision makers.

7. Land Allocation

Land allocated for use in accordance with its ecological characteristics may often be modified or transformed without loss of fertility. Sometimes its capability may be increased, as, by terracing and irrigation. It should, however, be recognized that the process may be irreversible so that initial misallocation or later mismanagement may permanently impair the value of the land. This underlines the need for environmental resource surveys to provide reliable data for successful land allocation.

Some of the types of knowledge required are:

(i)   natural area use—present vegetation and fauna, whether unique or representative of important eco-systems, intrinsic characteristics;

(ii) natural forests for timber production—present condition of the forest, potential for adequate regeneration:

(iii) plantation forestry and agriculture—climate and soil.

The real need is for positive and constructive management to reduce continuing damage and destruction as quickly as practicable. While awaiting comprehensive natural resources guidelines many

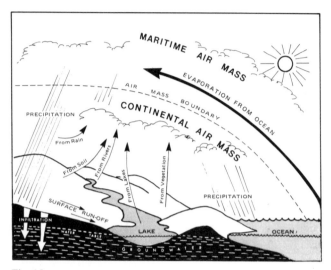

Fig. 15. HYDROLOGIC CYCLE. Solar energy continuously causes water to circulate throughout the biosphere, but the total quantity in all its forms is constant.

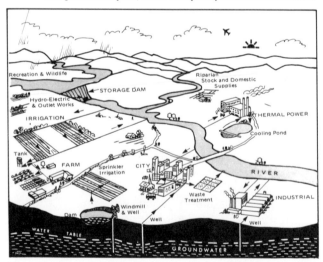

Fig. 16. WATER USES. Mankind's use of water for domestic, agricultural, industrial and other purposes does not diminish the amount in the water cycle. After use and treatment water returns to the world water bank.

Figs. 15 and 16. Water Resource Management Factors.

simple administrative actions can be taken. For instance, an administrative direction to permit the forestry agency to enforce existing illegal timber cutting laws would enable foresters to take practical action to reduce forest destruction and increase forest resources in real terms: that is to maintain the forest capital. Similar beneficial directions could be made about other resources such as grasslands and fisheries where a decentralized enforcement agency exists in most cases.

It can be seen from the foregoing, that an integrated resource management concept tends to bind together activities which are most frequently administered in isolation within "single mission" or government organizations. To co-ordinate the agencies of resource management, it is necessary to consider a process called for convenience "environmental planning", which treats the component parts (investments, output of useful goods and services, and resource supplies) as building blocks in the construction of human betterment programmes.

Selected Bibliography

Habitat Systems

Holling, C. S. *Resilience and Stability of Ecological Systems.* International Institute for Applied Systems Analysis (IIASA), Laxenburg, Austria. 1973.

Holling, C. S. *Description of Predation Model: Predatory-Prey Functional Response.* International Institute for Applied Systems Analysis (IIASA), Laxenburg, Austria. 1973.

Fiering, Myron B., and Holling, C. S. *Management and Standards for Perturbed Ecosystems.* International Institute for Applied Systems Analysis (IIASA), Laxenburg, Austria. 1974.

Soil

The International Conference on Desertification. Report. United Nations Environment Programme, Nairobi, Kenya. May 1977.

Eckholm, Erik P. *Losing Ground. Environmental Stress and World Food Prospects.* W. W. Norton & Co., Inc., New York. 1976.

Water

Man-made Lakes as Modified Ecosystems. SCOPE 4. International Council of Scientific Unions. Paris. 1972.

Water Conservation and Irrigation Commission. *Water Resources of the Hawkesbury Valley.* Prepared under the direction of J. G. Beale, Minister for Conservation, New South Wales, Sydney, Australia. 1973.

Water Resources Council. *Establishment of Principles and Standards for Planning— Water and Related Land Resources.* Federal Register. Vol. 38, No. 174. U.S.A. September 10, 1973.

Organization for Economic Co-operation and Development. *Water Management and the Environment.* OECD, Paris. 1973.

Department of Water Resources. *The California Water Plan. Outlook in 1973.* Bulletin No. 160–74. California, U.S.A. 1974.

Reynolds, Peter J. *Environmental Indicators in River Basin Management.* Proceedings of Tokyo Symposium. International Association for Scientific Hydrology. Tokyo, Japan. December 1975.

International Union for Conservation of Nature and Natural Resources. *An International Conference on Marine Parks and Reserves.* Proceedings. 12–14 May 1975. IUCN, Morges, Switzerland.

Biswas, A. S., (Ed.). *Systems Approach to Water Management.* McGraw-Hill Book Company, New York. 1976.

United Nations. *Report on the 1977 World Water Conference.* U.N., New York. 1977.

Forests

Hoffman, Thilo W. *The Sinharaja Forest.* Wildlife and Nature Protection Society, Colombo, Sri Lanka. 1972.

International Union for Conservation of Nature and Natural Resources. *Ecological guidelines for development in tropical forest areas of South East Asia.* IUCN occasional paper No. 10. Morges, Switzerland. 1973.

National Parks

Second World Conference on National Parks. Proceedings. 18–27 September 1972. Published for the National Parks Centennial Commission by the International Union for Conservation of Nature and Natural Resources, Morges, Switzerland. 1974.

Forster, Richard R. *Planning for Man and Nature in National Parks.* IUCN, Morges, Switzerland. 1973.

Franson, Robert T. *The Legal Aspects of Ecological Reserve Creation and Management in Canada.* International Union for Conservation of Nature and Natural Resources, Morges, Switzerland. 1975.

International Union for Conservations of Nature and Natural Resources. *An International Conference on Marine Parks and Reserves.* Proceedings. 12–14 May 1975. IUCN, Morges, Switzerland.

Parks Magazine. Published by Parks Canada and the National Park Service of the United States in collaboration with FAO, UNESCO and the Organization of American States (OAS), and with the co-operation of the Commission on National Parks and Protected Areas (IUCN) and Regional Advisers throughout the world. National Park Service, United States Department of the Interior, Washington, D.C., U.S.A.

Economics

Seneca, Joseph, and Taussig, Michael. *Environmental Economics.* Prentice Hall Publishing, Trenton, New Jersey. 1974.

Maler, Karl-Foran. *Environmental Economics.* Johns Hopkins University Press, Baltimore, Maryland. 1974.

Pearce, D. W. *The Economics of Natural Resource Depletion.* MacMillan, London. 1975.

Peterson, Frederick, M., and Fisher, Anthony C. *The Economics of Natural Resources.* University of Maryland Press, U.S.A. 1976.

Pearce, D. W. *Environmental Economics.* Longman, London. 1976.

Guidelines

International Union for Conservation of Nature and Natural Resources. *Ecological guideline for development in Tropical Forest Areas of South East Asia.* IUCN occasional paper No. 10. Morges, Switzerland. 1973.

Forster, Richard R. *Planning for Man and Nature in National Parks.* IUCN, Morges, Switzerland. 1973.

McEachern, John A., and Towle, Edward L. *Ecological Guidelines for Island Development.* IUCN Publication Series. No. 10. Morges, Switzerland. 1974.

General

Khambanoda, Charlermrath. *Thailand's Public Law and Policy for the Conservation and Protection of Land with Special Attention to Forests and Natural Areas.* The National Institute of Development Administration, Bangkok, Thailand. 1972.

Poore, M. E. D. *A conservation viewpoint.* Proc. R. Soc., London. A. 339, 395–410. 1974.

Franz, H., and Holling, C. S. *Alpine Areas Workshop.* 13–17 May 1974. International Institute for Applied Systems Analysis (IIASA), Laxenburg, Austria.

Smith, D. F., and Hill, D. M. *Natural and Agricultural Ecosystems.* Journal of Environmental Quality, 4 (2). 1975.

Maglen, L. R. *Non-renewable Resources and the Limits of Growth: Another Look.* Search. Vol. 8, No. 5. 1977. Canberra, Australia.

Nature and Resources Magazine. Official Bulletin of: the Man and Biosphere Programme, the International Hydrological Programme, and the International Geological Correlation Programme. UNESCO, Paris.

Odum, E. P. *Fundamentals of Ecology.* W. B. Saunders Co. 1971.

Watt, K. *Principles of Environmental Science.* McGraw Hill, New York. 1973.

Nelson, Michael, *The Development of Tropical Lands: Policy Issues in Latin America.* Johns Hopkins University Press, Baltimore, Maryland. 1973.

CHAPTER 12

Environmental Planning

1. Environmental Development Planning

"Strengthening pollution control! Reinforcing management of natural resources! They're still only bits of the whole issue; why isn't it all planned ahead?" Increasingly this is heard, and it's a healthy sign. Even more heartening is the progressive emergence of systems of *environmental planning*, that is, more effective planning for now and the future within environmentally dictated confines.

In recent years planning in many areas, including developing countries, has exhibited a welcome trend away from purely *economic* towards *economic and social* development. Scant attention however is yet given to the essential environmental component. This is so in national, regional and subregional planning, and also is reflected in many international aid programmes where *dollar effectiveness* so often subsumes *environmental effectiveness*.

Many learned papers and discussions at conferences on "national development" continue to highlight isolationist thinking typical of the various specialized disciplines, such as law, finance, economics, engineering, physical planning, sociology and ecology. Increasingly these purist protagonists are attempting to think beyond the confines of their disciplines. Unfortunately, under challenge, they too often take refuge in their specialities.

An unfortunate tendency in planning circles is to envisage the environment in the sense of "nature", with the planning function related directly to "nature preservation". It is essential for planners

to view the environment in a wider sense. Environmental considerations in planning should take account of the likely effects of development on the natural environment (air and water quality, plant and
animal life, land forms), on mankind (human waste, garbage, noise,
floods, droughts, displaced populations, slums), and on man-made
developments (historic buildings, monuments, parks). The scene is
depicted in Fig. 17. Past planning has been based too often on
the assumption that the benefits from new development are so great
they more than compensate for any resulting environmental damage.
Fortunately there are signs of a growing awareness that the consequences of human activities are more extensive than they have
appeared. For example, draining and filling swamps might provide
land for building but upset the delicate balance between wet land
and dry land habitats and intensify flooding. A new highway might
initially improve traffic flow but increase air and noise pollution
by attracting more vehicles. Increased recreational facilities might
result in increased public enjoyment but result in deterioration of
parklands, lakes and foreshores due to greater "people pressures".

People wanting a better environment for their homes should understand the choices confronting them. What kind of improved environmental quality do they want? How can it be paid for? Who will
pay? Old built environments are part of the cultural heritage. What
should be retained? How could this be done? What inconvenience
can be tolerated to achieve this? How much new building might
be absorbed in an area without destroying its essential quality?

Environmental planning implies a forward-looking process in
which all of the consequences of a proposed development are considered. These can only be assessed when there is an understanding
of the total environment and of the relationship between its components. Balanced consideration must be given to economic, technical,
social and ecological aspects. One way of achieving this is through
an environmental planning process shown in Fig. 18. The implementation of a complete planning system can be costly in demands
for funds, equipment and skills. It should be appreciated, however,
that even a small step into the second stage depicted in the process
would be a tremendous step forward in planning, and for those
affected by planning activities.

CITY
quality human eco-system with minimal congestion, pollution, pressures and poverty; enjoying full cultural opportunities

TRADE
trade and commerce conducted with multi-lateral recognition of responsibility to safeguard the environment

TOWN
quality urban living style in countryside setting; enjoying cultural opportunities; efficient city access

INDUSTRY
efficient production of goods and services; maximum recycling to minimise amount of residual contaminants

VILLAGE
quality rural style living preserving ethnic and cultural mores; good roading and access to modern goods and services

GOODS
goods designed for efficient use and consumption; and for maximum recycling of materials remaining after product usage

HUMAN HABITAT
habitation styled for traditional living; designed suitably for local climate and setting

TRANSPORT
efficient public mobility with reduced noxious emissions and noise; minimum energy wastage and environmental degradation

RECREATION
readily accessible areas for active and passive enjoyment; safeguards to prevent extending the capabilities of fragile eco-systems

HUMAN ACTIVITIES
conducted with respect for political, cultural and ethnic mores; and with account for ecology, technology, sociology and economics

RESOURCE ALLOCATION
co-ordinated management of investment; goods output, services, and resource supplies; merging physical, social, economic and environmental goals in human betterment programmes

ENERGY
prudent usage of energy sources; timber, fossil fuels, solar, hydro; with respect for the total environment

MINING
minimum environmental disturbance and maximum landscape restoration; protection from heavy metal contamination; commitment to supplies for future generations

WATER
provision of clean water for public health and hygiene, industry and recreation; emphasis on re-use and environmental enhancement

HERITAGE
preservation of precious landscapes and seascapes, historic monuments, and cultural values

WILDERNESS
preservation of unique natural features, fragile environments, fauna, flora, with protection of endangered species

FORESTLANDS
conservation; catchment protection, wild-life, recreation; and harvesting forest products on a sustained yield basis for preservation of natural forest capital

GRASSLANDS
development of the productive potential of grasslands; controlled grazing and firing; with safeguards to prevent environmental degradation

DESERTS
improving desert environments by application of modern management and technology

ENCLOSED FARMING & GRAZING
management of stocking rates to maintain productive harmony with the environment

INTENSIVE FARMING
high output with continuous preserva-tion of natural soil capital; safeguards to minimise environmental contamination

FOOD
availability of whole-some food; freedom from contamination and malnutrition

WETLANDS
conservation of wetland environments; protection of migratory birds, estuarine fisheries resources

OCEAN
conservation of fish, plants, minerals; harvesting; prevention of marine contamina-tion from land, water-way and ocean sources; endangered species protected

Environmental development planning is a continuous management process which aims to provide better opportunities for maximum community access to the products of national physical, cultural, social and economic environments. The emphasis is on planning with nature, for people, with their participation, to enhance human well-being through the efficient merging of the human "built environment" with the biosphere.

Fig. 17. Enhanced Human Well-being—the Product of Environmental Development Planning (elaborated from Beale 1975).

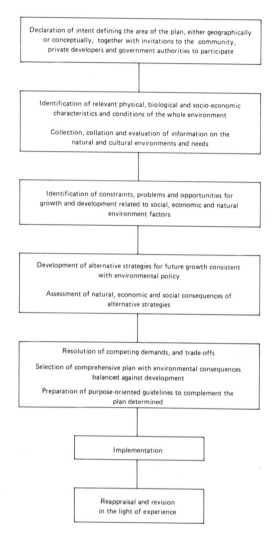

Fig. 18. Some Elements of an Environmental Development Planning Process
(*elaborated from Beale 1975*).

From the results seen in every country, most existing planning systems seem incapable of taking adequate account of environmental concepts. Traditional economic planning processes give little attention to the environment; conventional physical planning processes lack an environmental regard. They present no discernible human face to the environment.

It is possible to inject an environmental dimension into the general planning process by:

- becoming familiar with environmental planning techniques;
- making environmental analyses part of the planning system; and
- considering assessments of likely environmental consequences of individual proposals before decisions are made.

The effect of adding an environmental dimension to conventional technical-feasibility and economic-viability screening of a project or programme is illustrated diagrammatically in Fig. 19. This and other aspects of environmental planning are discussed in greater detail in the following subsections dealing with Economic Development Planning and Land-Use Planning.

2. Decision Making

a. *Political Decision Making*

"We can't even get a decision", people say. "How do you get politicians to make decisions?" This is an understandable sentiment.

Environmental planning, as has been seen earlier, calls for a greater effort from environmental managers to think problems through. Political decision-making is every bit as important as the technical decision the planner makes. First, it should be understood that politics is a science dealing with the form, organization and administration of a state, or part of it. Politicians at all governmental levels are practitioners. They might be members of a cabinet, an elected congress, or a provincial, municipal or village council. They

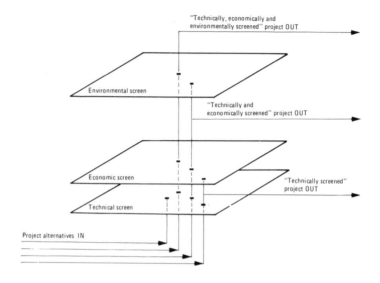

Fig. 19. Effect of Adding an Environmental Dimension to Conventional
Technical Feasibility and Economic Viability Screening of a Project.

could be ministers, administrators of agencies, departments or divisions at any governmental level.

Politicians are expected to resolve public issues concerned with the operation of the State. To do this, they explore for ideas they can promote. They float them to catch the drift of opinion. They study the issues looking for options rather than single solutions and then test these options with those whom they represent.

In making a decision a politician avoids getting mixed in detail, whereas an expert is heavily involved in detail. A politician seeks a wide range of opinions, where an expert concentrates on known specialist advice. Having made a decision, he tries to time his move to implement it in a way which will ensure that the governmental machinery can deliver a result which is acceptable. His survival depends on his success. Politicians are nothing new—mankind over the ages has depended greatly on their skills.

b. Crystal Ball Gazing

"The programme has bogged down again", the dejected bureaucrat said. "We just don't know what's going to happen. It's as if we don't even think the same way." Bureaucrats have said that about politicians since politicians first employed them.

Planners and administrators are constantly making judgements about the future. It is important for them to appreciate how they and others fit into the forecasting modes available. According to Hetman (1973) these are basically six, as shown in Fig. 20. Also, their applications from the administrative viewpoint are indicated.

A political agency head is likely to rely heavily on *prediction* modes, supported at times by selective use of *prospective investigation* modes. The bureaucracy will be more inclined towards systematic approaches, for example *forecasting* and *central planning* modes. Technical management units are likely to favour modes such as *projection* and *programming by objective*.

Planners and administrators need to realize that groups vary in the way they approach the future. They should be familiar with the differing methodologies which can be used to ensure effective pre-planning and be aware that their political bosses use crystal balls of other brands.

c. Decision-making Time Scales

"The politicians took little notice of our advice", the disenchanted specialist complained. "No notice of all our research." This happens all the time. When it is said it usually highlights the specialist's naivity about politics. Politics, which has been called "the art of the possible", connotes a time scale and a capacity to assess disparate sources of advice—what is possible is often less than perfection.

The usual gap between the politician and specialist is well illustrated in the following comment by Budowski of IUCN (1974) on Sir Otto Frankel's time scales which are shown in Fig. 21. "The gap between the politician and the genetical conservationist cannot be presented more eloquently, and yet those who know the facts desperately need to communicate with politicians and to establish

MODE OF APPREHENDING THE FUTURE	LOGICAL APPROACH	UNDERLYING OR EXPLICIT ASSUMPTIONS	PRINCIPAL GROUPS OF METHODS	ADMINISTRATIVE APPLICATIONS
Prediction	Subjective	Non-specified Non-explicit	Visionary statement Intuitive analogy	"Education" of the public, *e.g.* prohibition of littering, smoking, etc.
Forecasting	Probabilistic	Constant Contextual Situation	Extrapolation Correlation Multi-regression Statistical models	Trends; energy, natural resource consumption, price of commodities, etc.
Projection	Conditional	Constant Socio-economic Impact	Correlation Mathematical models Sensitivity analysis Simulation	Infrastructure needs, effects of rising population or affluence, estimation of consumer preferences as for housing or schooling, etc.
Prospective investigation	Exploratory Imaginative	Constant or given objectives	Opinions of experts Creativity groups Simulation models Exploratory models	Co-ordination of policy, appraisal of new technology, public opinion or reactions, etc.
Central planning	Normal or authoritative	Single and constant socio-economic system	Statistical models Mathematical models Iterative models	Nation-wide planning, phasing of major resource development, costs of environmental proposals, etc.
Programming by objective	Decisional	System-determined alternatives	Systems analysis Decision modelling Simulation Cross impact analysis	Policy change determination as in moving to better pollution controls or evaluating effect of environmental controls on natural resource exploitation, etc.

Fig. 20. Basic Modes of Apprehending the Future (*after Hetman 1973*).

PERIOD	OPERATION	OBJECTIVE	TIME SCALE OF CONCERN
To 8000 B.C.	Hunter-gatherer	Next meal	1 day
8000 B.C. –A.D. 1850	Peasant farmer	Next crop	1 year
1850–1977	Plant breeder	Next variety	10 years
1900–1977	Crop evolutionist	Broader genetic base	100 years
1977	Wildlife conservationist of gene pools	Dynamic wildlife conservation	10,000 years
Since the beginning	Politician	Current public interest	Next election

Fig. 21. The Time Scale of Concern for Wildlife and Plant Ecology (*after Budowski 1974*).

better lines of contact with decision makers as well as with the public in general."

Some issues of importance are beyond the horizons of present political concern. This makes it even more important for the various experts and bureaucrats to maintain their perspectives relative to the perspective which is natural to the political process with its built-in time scale. Very often the politician has to act now within an extremely short-term time scale dictated by public opinion.

3. Economic Development Planning

a. *Economics and the Environment*

"There is just too much notice taken of the economic viewpoint", environmentalists lament. There are, of course, good reasons for taking full account of economic thought in development. Economics is after all the social science which examines important aspects of daily life: mankind in earning and spending income, people and nations in wealth-getting and wealth-using activities. It seeks solutions to the general economic problem of relative scarcity—the gap between wants (not needs) and resources.

Put simply, an economy is a collection of socio-political institutions through which a community gathers and allocates scarce resources in order to solve the many wants of members of the community in an ever-increasing degree. That is, an organization for "economising", reflecting its derivations in the Greek "house management". The economy has various sectors. Those considered as "closed" are private (households), business (firms) and public (governments). The "open" sector of the economy is made up of these three plus the rest of the world (imports/exports).

"Economizing" is seeking to solve problems of the "economy" through, firstly, making the best use of available resources and, secondly, allocating scarce resources that have alternative uses among many competing wants.

Types of economy vary, for example, capitalist and socialist. Also, these economic systems may be unplanned, partly planned or planned. In all cases, however, the functions of the economy are production, distribution, exchange and consumption of wealth, plus public finance, growth and development. It is important for these functions to be performed with some thought for the likely environmental consequences and they therefore call for good housekeeping.

Environmental problems are common to all economic systems. In fact, environmental deterioration is a by-product of regular economic activities. In each of its many forms it is related in a measurable way to some particular production, distribution, or consumption process. The quantity of carbon dioxide released in the air bears a definite relationship to the amount of fuel burned by individuals, by industries, by automobile engines; the discharge of polluted effluents into streams in linked directly to the output of petroleum, paper, steel, textiles, chemicals; the degradation of the land is related to the taking of timber, agriculture, mining, recreation.

The science of economics possesses sharp tools to analyse and to aid solutions to many diverse problems. However, economics alone does not necessarily offer answers to environmental problems.

The problems can pose questions about the relevance of the values on which economic prescription is based. So the administrator must see economics as offering only some of the framework and some of the tools for solving some environmental problems. The economist cannot place values on the preferences of succeeding generations. On his side, the environmental manager can only ensure that as many options as possible are open to succeeding generations.

It is essential therefore to ensure attention is given to the likely impacts on the environment of all economic factors and this is discussed below.

b. Basic Planning Parameters

There are of course many circumstances where substantial economic, social and environmental advantages can be achieved through environmental development planning. Some basic planning parameters are shown in Fig. 22, which diagrammatically emphasizes the clear-cut difference between development planning with and without consideration for the environment. They are described briefly below:

(i)   *Investment*—failure to provide small pollution control investment originally (*e.g.* a new industrial plant without pollution controls) can result in much higher future investment (*e.g.* antipollution devices), with associated environmental degradation, and as a consequence increase the unit cost of production.

(ii)   *Output*—increased production from one source (*e.g.* a factory) can cause pollution which reduces the output from another source (*e.g.* farming).

(iii–v) *Resource Supply*—in the absence of a plan for optimal use over a period of time, and due to the failure to use appropriate technology, there can be a reduction in the effective supply of a resource (*e.g.* a renewable resource—a plantation; or a non-renewable resource—a mine) which is basic to production.

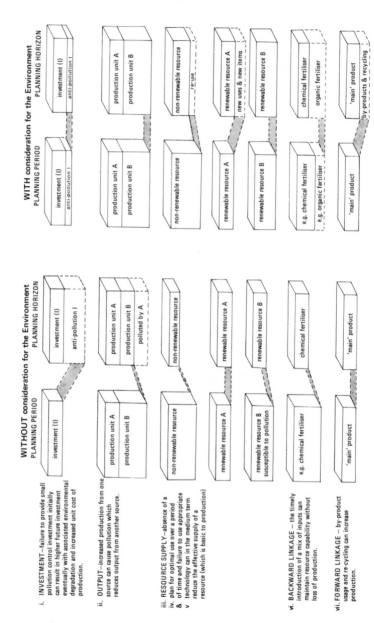

Fig. 22. Some Basic Planning Parameters *(elaborated from Suriyakumaran 1975, Beale 1975).*

(vi) *Backward Linkage*—the timely introduction of a mix of inputs (*e.g.* fertilizer and compost) can maintain resource capability (*e.g.* soil capability) without loss of production.

(vii) *Forward Linkage*—by-product usage and recycling can increase production.

The implementation of environmental development planning will lead to:

- Extension of the data base, that is provide greater knowledge of renewable and non-renewable resources. Additional data becomes available for environmental planning and as a bonus for scheduling sustained yields or long-term effective supply. (Past).
- Plans of action to optimize management of resources over a period of time resulting in the continued availability of resources on a sustained yield basis so that they are not exhausted by over-use or mis-use. (Present).
- Optimum use of all resources for development with sustained maintenance of future resource levels. (Future).

Environmental development should move through the following steps:

(i)   Specify objectives
(ii)   Establish criteria (operational objectives)
(iii) Formulate policies
(iv)   Develop options and evaluate implications
(v)   Select and prepare plans
(vi)   Determine priorities
(vii) Design programmes

It needs to take account of areas of human concern under environmental stress (see Appendix V) such as:

(i)   Economic and occupational status
(ii)   Social pattern or life style

(iii) Social amenities and relationships
(iv) Psychological features
(v) Physical amenities
(vi) Health
(vii) Personal security
(viii) Religion and traditional beliefs
(ix) Technology
(x) Cultural
(xi) Aesthetic
(xii) Political
(xiii) Legal
(xiv) Statutory laws and acts

Increasing rates of change in poverty, affluence, trade, technology, mobility and values are creating accelerated demands within a future of new and often bewildering possibilities. If environmental development planning is to respond properly to these changing needs there must be a continuous process of evaluation, review and feedback to assist today's planners and decision makers to make judgements which leave sufficient flexibility to take advantage of a variety of future options.

4. Economic Growth in Developing Countries

"We're trapped in a vicious circle of poverty. Our way out is through economic growth, not environmental control", said the harassed administrator of a developing country to a visiting environmental expert.

Two-thirds of the world's population live in economically under-developed countries in a state of poverty, and with an ever-present threat of starvation and illness. Malnutrition and disease keep the average life-span to about 30 years, less than half that in advanced countries.

The main characteristics of underdeveloped economies are poverty, overpopulation (with rapidly increasing population), subsistence production, dominance of low-productivity agriculture (employing 50%

or more of the work force), high illiteracy, inadequate education (including limited work-force skills), large inequality of income distribution, hampering customs, inefficient transportation, insufficient communication, and inadequate financial and government institutional systems. The net effect is in fact a vicious circle of poverty. The income of the majority, who are mostly poor, is used in merely staying alive. Savings are low, sometimes negative. In turn, investment of savings is low. The fundamental problem is that poverty tends to beget poverty.

It is not easy, especially where the population is rising quickly, to break out of this vicious circle of poverty. This can have deleterious environmental consequences, for restoration of environmental damage usually involves the use of manpower and materials, which is difficult to finance where an economy is static or going backwards.

Economic growth in developing countries can be considered in terms of several economic fundamentals, for example, population, natural resources, technology and investment.

Programmes to limit population are difficult to achieve when people are conditioned by custom to large families, or wish to be cared for in old age by their children. Development benefits are negated if economic gains fall short of the population increase, for then there can be no effective increase in real income per capita.

Many developing countries are poor in relation to natural resources. Land use reform may be necessary to ensure that land is used more effectively.

Developing countries have the advantage of imitating technology used in developed countries. This can often be much easier and less expensive than starting from scratch. However, the importation of advanced technologies can fail if there is a lack of adequate education and work skills, and also of the will to apply only appropriate technologies.

Developing countries usually find it is difficult to save and free resources for investment, most incomes being spent on surviving. Sometimes savings are diverted to non-productive purposes (*e.g.* grandiose projects—monuments, palatial buildings, unsuitable rural ventures). Also there are differing socio-economic results from investing in a capital-intensive project (building a dam in one year using machinery and 500 men) and one which is labour intensive (building this dam in ten years using 5000 men carrying materials in baskets).

The need is to ensure a reasonable balance between the numbers of people and available resources and progress towards this end could possibly be achieved through better economic and social development planning.

5. Economic Planning Process in Developing Countries

"That programme might be all right in a developed country, but will it work in our developing land?" the economic planner is often heard to ask.

Institutional problems concerning environmental management in less developed countries are usually due to the lack of "know-how" of planners and decision makers and to the misconception that environmental management necessarily impedes the process of development. Sometimes difficulties stem from governmental apathy. Others result from sectoral orientation of both planning and executive agencies concerned with the environment, together with overlapping responsibilities within *ad hoc* institutions.

a. Economic Development Planning Process

Many developing countries have established national economic planning agencies to control fund allocation. In this fiscal way they exercise a co-ordinating role in development. A simple version of a typical planning process is shown in Fig. 23. In this process the national development plan is devised by the central economic planning agency and is based on macro-economic analysis. This analysis takes into account (*a*) budget requests, (*b*) project submissions of executive agencies, (*c*) allocation of the development budget, and (*d*) preparation of the development plan. Individual executive agencies then implement development projects after budget appropriation (*e*). The screening is primarily economic.

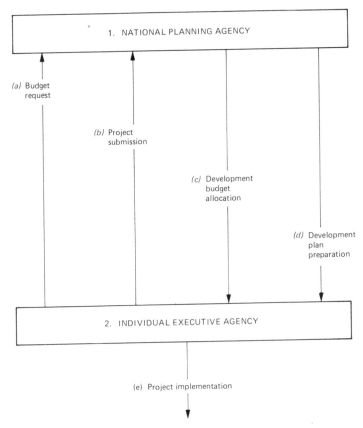

Fig. 23. Repetitive Process of National Economic Planning (simplified version, typical of many developing countries).

b. *Economic and Social Development Planning Process with Limited Environmental Input*

It is possible for a country to inject more environmental factors into its economic planning process by arranging for appropriate inputs from individual executive agencies. The prospects for achieving this are better where a traditional central "economic" planning

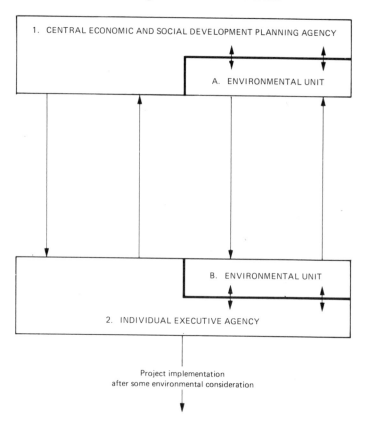

Fig. 24. Repetitive Process of Economic and Social Development Plan, Programme and Project Formulation with Limited Environmental Input (simplified version).

agency has already developed a "social" dimension. Also, where both the central planning agency and individual agencies have established environmental units.

A simplified version of this notion is shown in Fig. 24. The process could merely amount to discussions between environmental focal points in the central planning agency (1) and the responsible individual executive agency (2) concerning likely environmental consequences of projects and programmes. This approach could be strengthened by a government requirement that proposals transmitted to the central planning agency must include an environmental report, for example, an environmental impact statement.

As the diagram shows, small specialized environmental units A and B in both the "inputting" agency and the "receiving" agency (*i.e.* the central planning agency) are organized to ensure that proper translation of environmental advice occurs. For example, there are small environmental units established within Thailand's National Economic and Social Development Board (NESDB), and Philippines National Economic Development Authority (NEDA), and Venezuela's CORDIPLAN, which promote dialogue between themselves and appropriate governmental agencies.

c. *Economic and Social Development Planning with Integrated Environmental Input*

A government may desire to expand this idea by integrating environmental considerations with the national development planning process. One way to do this would be to add an Office of Environment to the simplified planning arrangement shown in Fig. 24, and simultaneously to strengthen the environmental unit in the central planning agency and extend those in the individual executive agencies. Thailand has achieved this through a National Environment Board (NEB), an environmental unit within its National Economic and Social Development Board (NESDB), and environmental focal points in some major national agencies.

A possible integrated planning process of the above mentioned type is shown in Fig. 25, and it could operate as follows:

(i) Project proposals, devised by an executive agency (2), are submitted to the Office of Environment (3) together with assessments of technical feasibility, economic viability, and environmental impact (*a*).

(ii) Proposals are reviewed environmentally by the Office and the result sent to the individual executive agency (*b*).

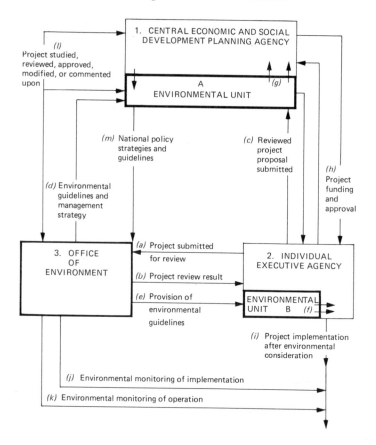

Fig. 25. Repetitive Process of Economic and Social Development Plan, Programme and Project Formulation with Integrated Environmental Input (simplified version).

(iii) The preferred project proposal is then submitted to the central planning agency (1) by the executive agency (2) for incorporation in the national development plan, and for funding (c):

(iv) To facilitate the process, the Office should prepare environmental guidelines for the central planning agency (*d*). These guidelines should also form part of a progressively evolving national environmental management strategy. The Office should also provide guidelines for individual executive agencies (*e*) to use in project formulation.

(v) The guidelines could then be used by the environmental units within executive agencies for project design and preliminary review prior to the submission being made to the Office (*f*) and (*a*) and/or the central planning agency (*f*) and (*c*).

(vi) The environmental unit (A) within the central planning agency (1) would then receive from the Office (3) the guidelines for project assessment (*d*) and receive proposals for environmental assessments prepared by the executive agencies (*c*).

(vii) After further review in the environmental unit of the central planning agency, within the scope of the guidelines, projects would then be considered for inclusion in the national economic plan, and for funding (*g*).

(viii) Projects after funding and approval by the central planning agency would be sent (*h*) to the executive agencies for implementation (*i*).

(ix) Environmental monitoring of both the implementation (*j*) and operation (*k*) of a project would be supervized by the Office to ensure compliance with the environmental approval constraints (*b*) and the guidelines (*d*) and (*e*).

(x) At times it may be necessary for the central planning agency to deal directly with the Office of Environment. This could involve two-way transactions including the study, review, modification and approval of a project or programme (*l*).

(xi) Projects and programmes are only part of a national development plan. It also includes policy, goals and strategy. There needs therefore to be interaction between the central planning agency and both the executive agencies and the Office of Environment on these matters (*m*). This is to ensure that the environmental strategy is compatible with the overall national planning approach of the government.

It is worthy to note that with input from the National Environment Board (NEB) the National Economic and Social Development Board (NESDB) has provided an environmental component in the Fourth Five-Year Plan (1977–1981) of Thailand.

d. *An Office of Environment in Economic Development Planning*

The above-mentioned process, designed to inject environmental planning into the overall economic development planning machinery, indicates some of the essential functions of an Office of Environment in this context, namely:

(i) environmental policy formulation and advice within the over-all national policy;

(ii) environmental strategy preparation compatible with the objectives of the national development plan;

(iii) environment initiatives in project and programme formulation, implementation and operation, for example:

(a) Preparation of environmental guidelines;

(b) Review and recommendations on environmental impact assessment; and

(c) Monitoring of project implementation and operation.

As indicated previously, many governments need to expand the environmental dimension in their development planning and administration. The review above shows that in order to achieve this it is essential to establish a "visible focal point" in the bureaucracy where environmental matters are kept under consideration. The focal point can range from a cabinet subcommittee, to a small group of experts in the office of the chief executive of the government, to a unit within a planning or executive agency, to a full-time minister and a major environmental agency, as discussed in Chap. 6. It is for a government to decide administrative options to best fit its own particular needs.

Environmental development planning as outlined above also shows the necessity for environmental focal points within relevant executive agencies. It must be emphasized that no matter what type of environmental office is established, to be effective, it must be charged with responsibility for ensuring consideration of likely environmental consequences at the planning stage. In carrying out this task it should play a reviewing role and therefore it should not prepare the original environmental impact assessment for a project or programme. The responsibility for preparing an environmental impact assessment should be placed on the executive agency sponsoring a project or programme. Also, the assessment must be done by the executive agency simultaneously with the preparation of its technical feasibility and economic viability studies.

A common misconception in both governmental and academic circles is that an impartial and objective assessment of the possible adverse environmental effects could not emanate from an individual sponsoring agency. Therefore, they argue, the assessment should be done by the environment office. It is just as likely that the environment agency would be biased in the other direction if it initiates the assessment. Even more usually, it lacks specialized knowledge. The mere fact that an agency examines the effects of its programmes on the surroundings will have the beneficial result of making the whole of its personnel aware of the agency's environmental responsibilities.

It should be appreciated that a project-sponsoring agency has the data on its projects. Also, environmental units within the agency structure should be capable of ensuring a competent assessment is made, and with experience it certainly should become of reliable standard. Furthermore, this internal exposure to environmental experience is educational and could flow on to project design, implementation and operation.

Experience has shown that during the introductory stage of a governmental environmental impact assessment scheme, assessments prepared by "developers" (governmental and private) usually contain more justification than analysis. The first efforts by "environmentalists" have the same failing. As time goes by the percentage of analysis tends to increase as the protagonists mature through discussion, debate, confrontation and education related to the conservation (wise use) of resources in the national interest.

It is emphasized that the environmental office must avoid getting bogged down in a pile of detailed work. Its task should be to devise ways for screening likely significant harmful environmental consequences. One way to achieve this is by having the environmental agency concentrate on the preparation of national environmental guidelines for both the planning and executive agencies to use in appraisals of their own activities. The position can be improved if the environmental agency prepares a national environmental strategy and if the national environmental objective is clearly defined in relation to other national objectives.

6. Land-use Planning

a. Land-use Planning Approaches

"If the economic planners don't spoil the countryside, the land-use planners are sure to. They never seem to listen to people." When this is said, and it often is, it is a sign of the lack of understanding between these planners and the community. And misunderstanding has resulted in much undesirable development.

The task of the land-use planner is to study all of the possibilities for land usage and provide realistic options to permit feasible growth and development to occur in conformity with the aspirations and needs of the community at large. It would therefore seem desirable to examine available land-use planning approaches.

Land-use guidelines can be an effective means of ensuring systematic consideration of important environmental aspects in the national planning process. In this way a national guideline for air quality would require that any area, where polluted air cannot be dispersed quickly, should not be zoned for industry with heavy emissions.

Environmentally oriented guidelines can provide a useful tool for regional and subregional planning. At the regional level, national guidelines can be translated into guidelines adapted to the particular needs of each region. Regional planning should take account of environmental aims (*e.g.* maintaining adequate oxygen levels in whole stretches of rivers and whole estuaries; the conservation of important regional ecosystems; preservation of historic localities). Regional planning can then indicate environmental capacities—the extent to which the development of various areas is compatible with the sum of individual environmental aims; environmental constraints—exclusion of specific types of development; and environmental standards—quality of air, water and noise emissions from industry.

At subregional levels, the emphasis should be more on specific parcels of land than on general policy, for example, how a particular park might be managed rather than on the general policy question of community open space requirements. These environmental problems of immediate concern to people are best dealt with, as far as possible, at the subregional level.

Effective application of environmental land-use planning approaches can help achieve a balance between the immediate satisfaction of the material needs of the community, the desire for economic and social progress and the conservation of valuable existing natural and man-made environments.

b. Land-use Planning Techniques

There are of course numerous land-use planning techniques ranging from intuitive to analytical to abstract. Many of these can be used to screen out likely harmful environmental impacts during the planning process. All methods have limitations so it may be necessary to use several methods in combination to ensure effective environmental screening.

In their paper "Nine Approaches to Environmental Planning", Robert H. Twiss and Ira Michael Heyman classify means of incorporating environmental information into land planning and decision making. Their nine models vary in their strengths and weaknesses and "the degree to which the outcomes of the planning decisions are prestated and thus predetermined".

The authors also state: "With a high degree of prestatement, residents, landowners, developers, visitors and environmentalists with a stake in land-use planning all have a more accurate picture of what a plan may entail and how it may impinge on their values. This aspect is especially important if land-use planning is to be opened up to a greater scrutiny and participation by the public. Finally, prestatement offers government officials the advantage of on-the-record land-use determinations that are less susceptible to behind-the-scenes political and economic pressure."

The first step is to appreciate the characteristics of land use planning technologies through the collection and review of information on the numerous techniques. This is presented below in descriptions of various methodologies with their application, strengths and weaknesses. It is possible to judge which techniques may be used with advantage in the environmental planning process. This provides the basis for administrative action to ensure that appropriate techniques are used by government agencies, private developers and individuals to screen proposals at the planning stage. The aim is to keep degrading environmental impacts minimal in every case and to achieve positive environmental improvement whenever possible.

From the viewpoint adopted in this publication the ideas of Twiss and Heyman do not cover the range of techniques completely. Accordingly their basic approach has been elaborated diagrammatically in Fig. 26, with particular advantages and disadvantages classified in Fig. 27. Techniques have been stratified into four groups for convenience in discussion, and also to indicate a fairly natural evolutionary sequence.

  A. *Anticipatory*—so called because the emphasis is on making the best first appraisal. Those within this grouping are:
     (1) background reports,
     (2) environmental impact statements, and
     (3) threshold analyses.
  B. *Standards*—so called because a "go/no-go" level is imposed on the environmental variable:
     (4) resource standards, and
     (5) multiple constraints.
  C. *Land Mapping*—which is self-explanatory:
     (6) unmapped land systems,
     (7) mapped land systems,
     (8) composite land capability maps,
     (9) two-map land capability planning, and
     (10) mapped master planning.

D. *Abstract*—so called to emphasize that the approach does not rely on tangibles like maps or set standards, but on a conceptualization of goals and objectives and reduction of these concepts to models, games or simulations:
(11) policy master planning, and
(12) simulated modelling and gaming.

1. Background Reports. A background report* is a collection, collation and evaluation of relevant existing information. (Refer to Figs. 26 and 27.) It is a well-known technique for commencing a study. Yet, too often its value is downgraded by administrators faced with complex environmental issues. A fairly natural predilection is to search for some more "scientific" technique—which often does not exist.

The collection, collation and evaluation of readily available data on the natural and cultural environments and human needs can assist in the identification of constraints, problems and opportunities for growth and development. These can be related to social, economic and natural environment factors because there will usually have been investigators of these aspects.

If information is collected with the co-operation of governmental agencies and other sources the result can be an unexpected co-ordination of information-gathering activities at all government levels and the identification of areas for specific studies. Furthermore, the unearthing of unpublished or forgotten reports is normal in compiling background information and therefore time can be saved when the need for later investigations becomes obvious.

A simple administrative decision to compile and analyse existing information can often overcome the inertia which is usual where more "scientific" methods are considered to be impracticable. In the resultant decision-making hiatus nothing happens. Information

---

* Useful examples of background reports are the *Hawkesbury River Valley Environment Investigation—Background Report. Phases I and II*, published under the authority of the Minister for Environment Control, New South Wales, in 1973, and *Alligator Rivers Study. A review report of the Alligator Rivers Region environmental fact-finding study*. C. S. Christian and J. M. Aldrick. Australian Government Publishing Service. Canberra 1977.

● ANTICIPATORY APPROACHES

1. BACKGROUND REPORT

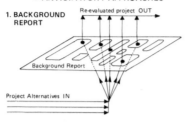

Re-evaluated project OUT

Background Report

Project Alternatives IN

NOTE: "Project" can sometimes include plan, proposal or programme.

● STANDARDS APPROACHES

4. STANDARDS

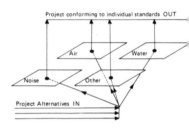

Project conforming to individual standards OUT

Air   Water

Noise   Other

Project Alternatives IN

2. ENVIRONMENTAL IMPACT STATEMENT

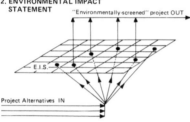

"Environmentally-screened" project OUT

E.I.S.

Project Alternatives IN

5. MULTIPLE CONSTRAINTS

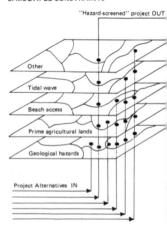

"Hazard-screened" project OUT

Other

Tidal wave

Beach access

Prime agricultural lands

Geological hazards

Project Alternatives IN

3. THRESHOLD ANALYSIS

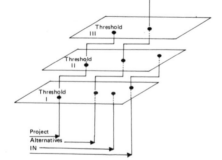

Feasible project OUT

Threshold III

Threshold II

Threshold I

Project Alternatives IN

Fig. 26 (pages 120–1). Illustration of Some Approaches to Land Use Planning (*after Robert H. Twiss and Ira Michael Heyman*).

● LAND MAPPING APPROACHES

6. UNMAPPED LAND SYSTEMS

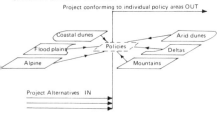

Project conforming to individual policy areas OUT

Coastal dunes
Arid dunes
Flood plains
Policies
Deltas
Alpine
Mountains

Project Alternatives IN

9. TWO-MAP LAND CAPABILITY PLANNING

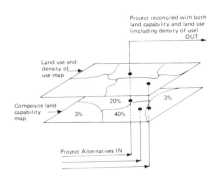

Project reconciled with both
land capability and land use
(including density of use)
OUT

Land use and
density of
use map

Composite land
capability
map

20%
3%
3%
40%

Project Alternatives IN

7. MAPPED LAND SYSTEMS

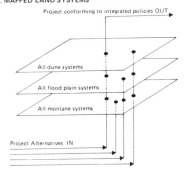

Project conforming to integrated policies OUT

All dune systems
All flood plain systems
All montane systems

Project Alternatives IN

10. MAPPED MASTER PLANNING

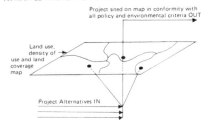

Project sited on map in conformity with
all policy and environmental criteria OUT

Land use,
density of
use and land
coverage
map

Project Alternatives IN

● ABSTRACT APPROACHES

11. POLICY MASTER PLANNING

8. COMPOSITE LAND CAPABILITY MAP

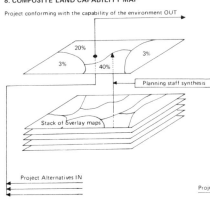

Project conforming with the capability of the environment OUT

20%
3%
3%
40%

Planning staff synthesis

Stack of overlay maps

Project Alternatives IN

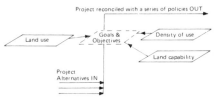

Project reconciled with a series of policies OUT

Land use
Goals &
Objectives
Density of use
Land capability

Project
Alternatives IN

12. SIMULATION AND GAMING

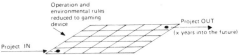

Operation and
environmental rules
reduced to gaming
device

Project OUT
(x years into the future)

Project IN

Some planning approaches and their strengths and weaknesses are classified to assist in the selection of the appropriate planning tools for use singly or in combination to deal with land use planning issues.

(A) ANTICIPATORY APPROACHES

(1) BACKGROUND REPORTS

A collection, collation and evaluation of readily available existing information on the natural and cultural environments and human needs, to assist in identification of constraints, problems and opportunities for growth and development related to social, economic and natural environmental factors.

Strengths:
- Can be quickly and inexpensively compiled with the co-operation of existing governmental agencies or other sources.
- Sufficient information is assembled to permit quick identification of many major issues and also indicate issues requiring further studies.
- Some pressing issues can be resolved on an ad hoc basis.
- Co-ordination of development can be introduced because many present and future development conflicts are visible.

Weaknesses:
- Inadequacies in data not always apparent.
- Until a data bank is provided background reports require regular reviews.
- Many issues will need further study.
- Basically non-directive.

(2) ENVIRONMENTAL IMPACT STATEMENTS

Ad hoc multi-disciplinary reviews to minimise the worst environmental problems of single projects.

Strengths:
- Capacity to intercept actions with significant environmental effects irrespective of the type, scope, purpose or origin.
- Evaluates alternatives including "do nothing".
- Project characteristics are sufficiently specified to facilitate detailed analysis of likely deleterious effects late in the decision process.
- "Educates" the proposer of a project who prepares it.

Weaknesses:
- Data is often qualitative or broadly comparative.
- Late review makes needed changes difficult (reviews must be done simultaneously with technical and economic studies).
- Range of alternatives tends to be narrow and recommended major changes could circumvent a realistic project in favour of a wise unspecified alternative.
- Estimating additive, cumulative, or growth-inducing effects is non-feasible without some broader planning structure because an E.I.S. in isolation is project specific.
- Burden of answering broad planning questions is placed on the proponent government agency or developer.

(3) THRESHOLD ANALYSES

Step by step analyses for defining development thresholds (i.e. physical limitations to growth) and the evaluation of the costs necessary to step over each threshold.

Strengths:
- Overcomes "linearity concept", because many environmental development decisions can only come in "steps" as indicated by threshold concept.
- Assists problem identification.
- Identifies cost to overcome growth limitations.
- Can be tested in the real world so that potentially erroneous planning conclusions are avoided.

Fig. 27 (pages 122–3). Classification of Some Approaches to Land Use Planning.

Weaknesses:
- Basically a problem anticipating technique because it is deficient in the parameters of a planning strategy.
- Can only serve as part of the array of analytic techniques of planning.
- Little leverage for imposing mitigating measures on marginally acceptable projects because criteria lead to "yes" or "no" decisions.
- Criteria in isolation are virtually inflexible, piecemeal decrees providing little opportunity for trade-offs between criteria which might lead to a higher net benefit to the environment.
- Estimating additive, cumulative and growth-inducing effects is non-feasible.
- Easily quantified environmental dimensions may override "softer" environmental "issues".

(B) STANDARDS APPROACHES

(4) RESOURCE STANDARDS

Comparisons of designs or performances against regulatory standards, with proposals satisfying existing regulations being presumed environmentally sound.

Strengths:
- Projects can be designed precisely to meet predetermined emission standards on sources of pollution.
- Compliance with standards can be readily policed.
- Being discrete, standards facilitate political debate and resolution.
- Standards are resistant to change in response to pressures which exist in important cases.

Weaknesses:
- Little leverage for imposing mitigating measures on marginally acceptable projects because standards lead to "yes" or "no" decisions.
- Discrete standards can oversimplify complex planning issues.
- Meaningful standards must be keyed to economic and technological realities, which often change more rapidly than standards.
- Standards in isolation are virtually inflexible, piecemeal decrees providing little opportunity for trade-offs between standards which might lead to a higher net benefit to the environment.
- Estimating additive, cumulative and growth-inducing effects is non-feasible.
- Easily quantified environmental dimensions may override "softer" environmental "issues".
- Setting realisitic standards and measuring performance relevant to them requires technological skills.

(5) MULTIPLE CONSTRAINTS

Studies to make developments more responsive to environmental hazards by checking aspects of each section of a project against the information on a series of maps depicting the location and intensity of environmental variables.

Strengths:
- Many varied environmental problems may be covered simultaneously.
- Developments in hazardous or sensitive areas can be more responsive to environmental problems.
- "Soft" environmental areas can be represented in the planning process.
- Maps can be keyed directly to regulations thereby providing a clear rationale.
- Trade-offs between environmental variables are apparent.
- Provides considerable flexibility.

Weaknesses:
- Predicting additive, cumulative and growth-inducing implications of multiple constraints is difficult (and there can be regions of no development).
- Dealing with the numerous overlay maps of specific parameters can cause planners computational and representational problems.
- Preparing and interpreting the data requires technological skills in quantity.

(C) LAND MAPPING APPROACHES

(6) UNMAPPED LAND SYSTEMS

Classifications of areas of land and water into similar types or zones (geology, soil, vegetation, climate, land form, and physical and biological processes) in order to specify "land systems" expressing interrelated environmental processes, constraints and opportunities.
Strengths:
- Approach is holistic and ecological, stressing known relationships.
- Guidelines can be geared to classifications describing environments.
- Policies and regulations can be made specific to likely environmental problems thereby facilitating the administration of policies.
Weaknesses:
- Flexibility remains in the definition of specific environmental units at the local level thereby increasing regional planning difficulties.
- Significant efforts in environmental inventory and analysis must precede the development process.

(7) MAPPED LAND SYSTEMS

Additional to the specification of environmental types or zones, as for the unmapped "land systems" approach, areas are depicted, usually at a regional level, in a series of maps classifying land as to land systems.
Strengths:
- Those of the "unmapped land systems" approach (6), plus:
- Mapping which makes the procedure more complete because developers, land owners and planners can see how regulations can work out on the ground.
- Forecast opportunities and constraint.
Weaknesses:
- Those of the "unmapped land systems" approach plus:
- More costly and time consuming.

(8) COMPOSITE LAND CAPABILITY MAPS

Synthesizing of constraint maps or land systems into a single "land capability" map expressing key environmental features.
Strengths:
- The "carrying capacity" of the land can be expressed in several levels of environmental robustness, from fragile land which cannot tolerate disturbance to land robust enough to absorb intensive development.
- Sites on which a development can be encouraged and places where development should not occur are indicated.
- Individual plans, developments and programmes can be tested against a map and the likely environmental impacts forecast quickly.
- Groups of experts and citizens can assist in the making of planning judgements.
Weaknesses:
- Large effort and cost in inventory and analysis needed.
- High technical skills required.

(9) TWO-MAP LAND CAPABILITY PLANNING

A technique to increase the specificity of "composite land capability" planning by using in addition a traditional land use/density map.
Strengths:
- Those of normal "land capability" planing (8), plus:
- Provides a two-map screen for project or plan proposals. The land use map indicates the possible locations of various uses; the land capability map governs in percentage terms the area that can be disturbed. The two maps together serve to give a fairly complete statement of the way in which a region can be permitted to develop.
Weaknesses:
- Requires a large input of time, effort, technical skill and funds for data, analysis and preparation.

- Completeness of prestatement precludes later flexibility in decision making.

(10) MAPPED MASTER PLANNING

A complete end statement representing the ultimate prestatement of policy as it affects land use. Traditionally a map in which all policy and environmental concerns are integrated into a final expression of permitted land use and density.
Strengths:
- Co-ordination is required between the master plan and the zoning plan so that the density or intensity of development is reflected in the land use map.
- Provides a complete picture which can be challenged and perfected.
- Can be subjected to environmental impact assessment because the policies are fairly visible.
Weaknesses:
- The master plan is sometimes seen as an ultimate goal and this is never achieved in the real world.
- An inflexible approach in attempting to decide today the ultimate future use.
- Lengthy preparation may make the plan out of date when implemented.
- High demands on time, effort, technological skills and funds;
- Can be subverted for speculative gains which upset marketplace data used in its compilation.

(D) ABSTRACT APPROACHES

(11) POLICY MASTER PLANNING

Specification of the goals and objectives or an area in a number of policy statements and regulations. Development objectives are compared with them and ad hoc decisions made.
Strengths:
- Provides an opportunity for flexible approaches.
- Few maps need to be prepared expressing the working out of policies and goals of an area.
- Proposals can be effectively evaluated in the light of goals related to specific developments, of other policies and of concessions required from developers to minimise environmental damage and promote welfare.
Weaknesses:
- Many policies are inclined to be "motherhood" statements.
- It is difficult for the public and developers to foresee the implications and conflicts inherent in the policy statements.
- "Eleventh hour" emergence of conflicts leads to delays while these unforeseen issues are worked out.

(12) SIMULATED MODELLING AND GAMING

Analyses based on assumptions that the various planning parameters will behave in a predictable manner.
Strengths:
- Various strategies can be tested, which is impossible in real life without committing resources.
- Time is compressed in gaming and simulation modelling, which thus become education tools for planners who would otherwise be unable to visualise all the major and side effects and their interactions over lengthy time periods.
- Excellent for informing policy-makers, developers and critics as to the complexities and relationships involved in decisions.
- Good public involvement tool.
Weaknesses:
- In real life the parameters may not behave as predicted, particularly in the medium and long term.
- Highly technical equipment and skills are needed.
- Even best available models are fairly crude, few have been validated, and integration of models not yet feasible.
- Predictive value variable.

is the basis of decision-making so that it is usual for some decisions to be possible if information for them has been compiled.

2. Environmental Impact Statements. An environmental impact statement (E.I.S.) is a technique for compiling and assessing the multi-disciplinary information needed to weigh the likely impact on its surroundings of a particular proposal. (Refer to Figs. 26 and 27.)

Environmental impact statements are therefore project-by-project reviews. They are used in an endeavour to minimize adverse environmental effects from specific developments. The assessments are usually qualitative and the potential impacts are judged against those expected from alternative proposals, including the alternative of doing nothing.

Environmental impact statements can be effective environmental screens for particular projects at local levels. They have limitations, for this technique rarely takes full account of additive, cumulative, or growth-inducing effects. Some factors may need checking by other methods to ensure adequate screening prior to a particular development being allowed to proceed.

At regional levels statements may sometimes be usefully applied to evaluate policies which are part of the broader planning process but sophisticated skills are needed to use E.I.S.'s in this way.

A model set of practical environmental impact guidelines is included as Appendix VI, and some useful references are listed in the Selected Bibliography.

3. Threshold Analysis. Threshold analysis according to Kozlowski *et al.* (1972) is a step-by-step procedure for defining those development thresholds which are very closely related to the physical limitations to growth. These limitations can relate to such factors as topography or regional geography. (Refer to Figs. 26 and 27.)

To overcome some particular types of limitations a markedly increased rate of investment must occur if developmental activities are to continue in an orderly manner without disrupting activities such as employment, provision of health and education facilities. Threshold analysis anticipates those steps where limitations will make their influence felt significantly.

Threshold analysis thus serves environmental planning by connecting it to the investment decisions which must be made before a land use plan can be feasible. The "linearity" (the assumption that all investment occurs in equal increments) of conventional planning is therefore overcome. Because of this, threshold analysis is basically a problem-anticipating technique which can only serve as part of the array of analytic techniques employed in planning. In this respect it is a more quantitative adjunct to background reports or certain aspects of environmental impact statements and a very valuable precursor of land capability methods.

4. Resource Standards. Environmental effects can be assessed against predetermined resource standards (*e.g.* the capacity of a river basin to absorb pollutants). In this technique relevant environmental aspects of a proposed development are compared with regulatory standards (*e.g.* air, water, noise). A proposal that satisfies existing standards is considered environmentally sound. (Refer to Figs. 26 and 27.)

This method can be a useful screening device. A deficiency is that standards tend to be set in isolation for individual aspects of the environment, making trade-offs between the various factors difficult. The implementation in isolation of a motor vehicle emission standard may upset road design, traffic flow or national energy policy: a water quality standard may make an agricultural land use prohibitively expensive and thereby jeopardize "green" space. Additive and cumulative effects are difficult to foresee. Further screening is usually necessary, but where a standard is in fact set the effect is to "buy time" until better techniques and resources can be marshalled. There is always the danger that the "mathematical" nature of a resource standard will divert attention from certain non-quantifiable parameters such as aesthetics.

5. Multiple Constraints. The multiple constraints approach is a higher level technique than the resource standards approach. Environmental factors for an area are mapped to show their location and intensity, much as the isohyets and isobars are mapped in meteorological charts. Features such as geological hazards, prime agricultural lands, beach access, tidal wave susceptibility or other hazards, can be represented on individual maps. These maps are used to assess developments against indicated environmental constraints. The maps can be keyed to laws, and development only permitted where the intensity of the environmental variable is sufficiently low, or where adequate measures are introduced to mitigate harmful environmental consequences. (Refer to Figs. 26 and 27.)

The effect of the multiple constraints system is to make development in hazardous and sensitive areas more responsive to public environmental concern. Using this method, it is possible to assess to a reasonable degree of accuracy the cost to developers and the community of safeguarding the environment and, ultimately whether development should be precluded altogether. For example, knowledge about earthquake fault zones or naturally unstable slopes can be applied usefully in city and town planning and building control: information on flood zones can assist in reducing flood damage and so save on the cost of flood control measures and community costs such as insurance or civil rehabilitation.

This approach allows a number of environmental factors to be covered simultaneously. Also "soft areas" such as scenic resource quality can be considered in the planning process. Possible trade-offs among environmental variables become apparent.

A disadvantage in common with the resource standards technique is the difficulty in foreseeing additive and cumulative effects. Dealing with a large stack of overlay maps can be a problem for planners. Sophisticated processing of data can be of assistance in this regard, although it can create its own problems with interpretation, the use of higher skills and higher costs.

6. *Unmapped Land Systems.* This approach is holistic and ecological and stresses known relationships. It recognizes the inter-relationship of environmental components, and the need to specify "land systems" as the basis for classifying environmental processes, constraints and opportunities. Lands and waters are classified into zones of similar geology, vegetation, climate, land form, and also by physical and biological processes such as susceptibility to erosion, sedimentation

or deposition (Figs. 26 and 27), much as an ecologist defines ecosystems.

Unmapped information can be used to make deductions about natural processes and valuable resources. Predictions can be made about likely responses to environmental impacts, and these can be improved as development proceeds.

Guidelines can be keyed to classifications (not maps) describing whole environments. The simple delineation of land systems can help planners who can easily envisage them from descriptions like "delta", "coastal dunes" or "flood plain". Policies and regulations can be made specific to likely environmental problems, thereby facilitating the administration of particular land use policies.

It is important to recognize that flexibility will remain in the definition of specific environmental units at the local level and this can increase regional planning difficulties. It is important to note that this approach, although not relying on maps, needs the support of an inventory before it can be used effectively. It is possible, however, to gain some benefits through the use of comprehensive background (inventory) reports cataloguing available data to produce land systems definitions of low, but useable, resolution.

7. Mapped Land Systems. Placing unmapped information onto maps vastly improves its usefulness and conceptualization for land-use planning. In effect similar environments (ecosystems) can be grouped according to existing land use, ecology, landform, etc., exactly as unmapped systems are classified and treated as subregional planning units.

It is possible to predict the reaction of such units to environmental disturbance because their boundaries do not change rapidly. Environmental consequences of development can be predicted with reasonable accuracy within the mapped units. Even more effort needs to be devoted to inventory as the land systems themselves have to be identified as repeating units within the landscape and their boundaries then mapped to scales exactly commensurate with planning maps.

8. Composite Land Capability Maps This advanced approach takes land planning a step farther. It involves the synthesizing of multiple-constraint maps and land-systems maps into a single "land-capability" map expressing key environmental features. This composite map specifies the percentage of land that can, for instance, be disturbed by various forms of development or perhaps covered with impervious surfaces. (Refer to Figs. 26 and 27.)

A way of achieving this is by overlaying available constraint maps and then, by assigning "weights" to the various constraints, designating those areas with the most problems for exclusion. Important technical and value judgements are "locked into" the plan at this point using this methodology. It is possible for groups of experts and citizens to assist in making these judgements.

The "carrying capacity" of the land can be expressed in several levels of robustness, which might range from zero for fragile land which cannot tolerate any disturbance (*e.g.* a rare species habitat) through several levels of environmental sensitivity to land robust enough to absorb intensive development such as an industrial area or to a metropolitan beach capable of absorbing enormous human pressures.

Planning guidelines at national, regional, and local levels can be based on land capability maps, to show positive and negative indications for development. Individual plans, developments and programmes can be tested against the map and the likely environmental impacts forecast quickly. The map can also be used to indicate the sites on which intensive development can be encouraged.

The technique can also be used to predict future land use and density, thereby ensuring that zoning plans take into consideration the total capacity of a particular environment. It should be noted that a large effort in inventory, preparation, and analysis is needed, augmented by sophisticated technical skills.

9. Two-Map Land Capability Planning. An approach that further increases levels of land-use planning specificity can be termed "Two-Map Land Capability Planning". In this technique socio-economic and land-use issues are considered separately from natural environment concerns. This is done by using conventional "land-use" and "density of land-use" maps in conjunction with a "Composite Land Capability Map" as described above. (Refer to Figs. 26 and 27.)

The land-use density map shows the location and density of permitted land uses where high- and low-density commercial, industrial, housing, recreation and other uses can go. The two-map composite land capability map governs in percentage terms the area that can be disturbed by development. The approach provides a two-map screen for project or plan proposals. The two maps taken together serve to give a fairly complete statement of the way in which a region will be permitted to develop.

A large input of time, effort, technical skill and funds for data, analysis and presentation is necessary to apply this technique.

10. Mapped Master Planning. The aim of this approach is to provide a complete end statement of policy as it affects land use. Traditionally, it is a map in which all policy and environmental concerns are integrated into a final expression of permitted land use and density of land use. (Refer to Figs. 26 and 27.)

In this method co-ordination is required between the master plan and a zoning plan so that the density or intensity of development is reflected in the land-use map. Also, a master plan provides a complete picture which can be challenged and perfected over time. Furthermore it can be subjected to environmental impact assessment because the policies are fairly "visible".

A master plan is sometimes seen as the ultimate goal and of course this is never achieved in the real world. It is a somewhat inflexible approach because it attempts to decide today the ultimate use of land for a long time ahead. Also, it can become a speculative "guidebook" which upsets the market-place data which will have been used in its compilation.

This method makes heavy demands on time, effort, technological skills and funds. If the preparation is lengthy the plan may be out of date when it is implemented.

Useful references are the master plans prepared from time to time for the great cities of the world.

11. Policy Master Planning A simpler but abstract master planning approach is through the specification of the goals and objectives of an area in a number of policy statements and regulations. Development objectives are compared with them and ad hoc decisions made. For example, a housing proposal could be evaluated in relation to goals such as for open space, transportation, education. Also proposals can be evaluated in the light of concessions required from developers to minimise environmental damage and promote welfare. (Refer to Figs. 26 and 27.)

Few maps need to be prepared expressing the working-out "on the ground" of policies and goals in the area. Opportunities are thus provided for the flexibility essential to effective planning.

It should be understood, however, that many policies are inclined to be in the nature of "motherhood" statements. Further, it is difficult for the public and developers to foresee the implications and conflicts inherent in policy statements. Often they do become aware of "situations" late in the planning process and delays are then necessary to resolve matters at issue.

12. Simulated Modelling and Gaming Further abstraction is possible through simulated modelling and gaming which rests on assumptions that various planning parameters will behave in a predictable manner. (Refer to Figs. 26 and 27.)

This approach permits various strategies to be tested in a manner impossible in real life without committing substantial resources or making irretrievable development decisions.

Time is compressed in gaming and simulation modelling. Games and models thus become educational tools for planners who would otherwise be unable to visualize all the major and minor side-effects and interactions over lengthy periods. Critics, developers and other interest groups are able to interact in the same "educational" context.

It should be recognized, however, that in real life, planning parameters may not behave as predicted, particularly over the medium and long term. Also, while some gaming devices can be simple, this technique usually requires highly technical equipment and skills to design and construct games and to mount visual displays of their outcome.

c. Administrative Usage of Approaches to Land-Use Planning

It will be seen from the foregoing examples that a wide range of land-use planning techniques is available. It will also be appreciated that they can be used singly or in combination to screen projects and plans for likely environmental impacts, to modify them, and in some cases to encourage actions which will enhance the environment.

Naturally, a professional planner will be interested in the technical aspects of the various approaches. But he should also be interested in ways to use this technology effectively in environmental planning and to influence subsequent management.

The administrator must appreciate land-use planning methods, although his special interest will be to see how the various techniques rank as administrative tools. He requires an indication of the strengths and weaknesses of the approaches in policy, programme and project planning at national, regional and local levels. He wants to know what resources are needed—funds, skills, equipment. He needs an idea of the ease of understanding of techniques— by specialists, administrators and laymen severally, and in communication with each other

The various methods outlined should at least indicate to planners and administrators whether the best available methods have been used and also whether major possibilities have been exhausted. Where an administration is feeling its way into environmental planning it is worthwhile distinguishing simple from complex techniques which might exhaust or commit available resources before anything positive is achieved. Figure 28 indicates some possible administrative areas of interest on a comparative basis.

No matter what systems and techniques are used in planning there is always a constraining environment—the environment of realism. In the contexts being explored in this publication the component parts of that realism can be extracted for examination— the critical realities of population, food supplies and energy.

INDICATORS FOR ADMINISTRATIVE USAGE

--	low
-	low—medium
0	medium
+	medium—high
++	high

To assist in the selection of appropriate planning tools for use singly or in combination

APPROACH	CRITERION															
	Policy Planning			Programme Planning			Project Planning				Resources Needed			Ease of Understanding		
	National	Regional	Local	National	Regional	Local	National	Regional	Local	Individual	Funds	Skills	Equipment	Specialist	Administrator	Layman
A. Anticipatory:																
(1) Background Reports	--	0	0	--	0	0	--	+	+	+	--	--	--	++	++	++
(2) Environmental Impact Statements	--	-	-	--	-	-	-	-	+	+	--	--	--	++	++	++
(3) Threshold Analyses	0	+	++	0	++	++	-	0	0	-	0	+	0	+	+	-
B. Standards:																
(4) Resource Standards	-	-	0	-	+	+	-	0	+	++	0	0	+	++	++	0
(5) Multiple Constraints	0	+	++	-	0	+	-	0	+	++	+	++	0	++	+	0
C. Land Mapping:																
(6) Unmapped Land Systems	0	+	+	0	+	+	0	+	+	+	0	+	0	+	+	0
(7) Mapped Land Systems	+	+	+	+	+	+	+	+	+	+	+	+	+	+	+	0
(8) Composite Land Capability Maps	+	+	++	+	+	+	+	+	+	+	++	++	++	++	+	-
(9) Two-Map Land Capability Planning	++	++	++	++	++	++	++	++	++	++	++	++	++	+	+	-
(10) Mapped Master Planning	++	+	0	0	0	0	+	+	+	+	++	++	++	+	++	-
D. Abstract:																
(11) Policy Master Planning	++	0	-	0	0	0	0	0	-	-	+	+	+	+	++	--
(12) Simulated Modelling and Gaming	0	0	0	0	+	+	0	+	++	++	+	++	+	0	+	--

Fig. 28. Administrative Strengths and Weaknesses of Some Approaches to Land Use Planning.

Selected Bibliography

Environmental Development Planning

Alonso, W. *Problems, purposes and implicit policies in national strategy in urbanisation.* Institute of Urban and Regional Development, working paper 158. University of California, at Berkeley, Calif., U.S.A. 1971.

Meltsner, A. *Political Feasibility and Policy Analysis.* Public Administrative Review, Vol. XXXII, December 1972.

Rittel, Horst W. J., and Webber, Melvin M. *Dilemmas in a General Theory of Planning.* Policy Sciences 4, 155–169. 1973. Elsevier Scientific Publishing Company. Amsterdam. The Netherlands.

Beale, J. G. *Pause-Plan-Protect: from Slogan to Environmental Impact Policy.* Paper to the Spring Conference on the Professions and the Built Environment, 2–3 May 1974. The Harvard Graduate School of Design, Harvard University, Cambridge, Mass., U.S.A.

Scott, Randall W., *et al. Management & Control of Growth: Issues. Techniques. Problems. Trends.* Volumes I, II and III. The Urban Land Institute, Washington, D.C., U.S.A. 1975.

Reitze, Arnold W., Jr. *Environmental Planning: Law of Land and Resources.* North American International, Washington, D.C., U.S.A. 1974.

Suriyakumaran, C. *Environment and Development Planning.* Regional Office for Asia and the Pacific. United Nations Environment Programme, Bangkok, Thailand. 1976.

Decision Making

Jantsch, Eric. *Technological Forecasting in Perspective.* OECD, Paris. 1967.

Chisholm, Roger, K., and Whitaber, Gilbert R., Jr. *Forecasting Methods.* Irwin Publishers, London. 1971.

Brubaker, Sterling. *To Live on Earth.* Resources for the Future, Inc., the Johns Hopkins University Press, Baltimore, Maryland, U.S.A. 1972.

Hetman, Francois. *Society and the Assessment of Technology.* Organisation for Economic Co-operation and Development, Paris. 1973.

Coomber, N. H., and Biswas, Asit K. *Evaluation of Environmental Intangibles.* Genera Press, Bronxville, New York. 1973.

Budowski, Gerado. *Should Ecology Conform to Politics.* The International Union for the Conservation of Nature and Natural Resources, Morges, Switzerland. 1974.

Beale, J. G. *Pause-Plan-Protect: from Slogan to Environmental Impact Policy.* Paper to the Spring Conference on the Professions and the Built Environment, 2–3 May 1974. The Harvard Graduate School of Design, Harvard University, Cambridge, Mass., U.S.A.

134   *The Manager and the Environment*

Matthews, William H. *Resource Materials for Environmental Management and Education.* The M.I.T. Press, Cambridge, Mass., U.S.A. 1976.

Economic Growth in Developing Countries

Office of the President, Caracas. *4th Plan of the Nation.* (1970–75). Venezuela. 1970.
Office of the President, Caracas. *5th Plan of the Nation.* (1975–80). Venezuela. 1975.
Office of the Prime Minister, Bangkok. *The Third Economic and Social Development Plan.* (1972–76). Thailand. 1972.
Office of the Prime Minister, Bangkok. *The Fourth Five-Year Plan.* (1977–81). Thailand. 1977.
Office of the President, Manila. *Four-Year Development Plan.* (1974–77). The Philippines. 1974.
Office of the Prime Minister, Colombo. *The Five-Year Plan.* (1972–76). Sri Lanka. 1972.
Office of the Prime Minister, Colombo. *Review of the Five-Year Plan and Revised Development Programmes.* (1975–77). Sri Lanka. 1975.

Economic Development Planning

Organisation for Economic Co-operation and Development. *Problems of Environmental Economics.* OECD, Paris. 1972.
Organisation for Economic Co-operation and Development. *The Polluter Pays Principle.* OECD, Paris. 1975.
Organisation for Economic Co-operation and Development. *Pollution Charges. An Assessment.* OECD, Paris. 1976.
World Bank. *Environmental, Health and Human Ecological Considerations in Economic Development Projects.* Washington, D.C., U.S.A. 1974.
Holmes, Nicholas (Ed.). *Environment and the Industrial Society.* Hodder & Stoughton, London. 1976.
Leontief, Wassily. *The Future of the World Economy* (extract). A United Nations Study. Oxford University Press, New York. 1977.
Organisation for Economic Co-operation and Development. *Environmental Damage Costs.* OECD, Paris. 1974.
Organisation for Economic Co-operation and Development. *Problems in transfrontier pollution.* OECD, Paris. 1974.
Organisation for Economic Co-operation and Development. *Economic measurement of environmental damage.* OECD, Paris. 1976.
Organisation for Economic Co-operation and Development. *Economics of transfrontier pollution.* OECD, Paris. 1976.
Banks. Harvey O., *et al. Water Resource Planning.* National Water Commission, NTIS, Springfield, Virginia, U.S.A. 1970.

James, L. Douglas and Lee, Robert R. *Economics of Water Resources Planning.* McGraw-Hill Book Co., New York. 1971.

James, L. Douglas (Ed.). *Man and Water, The Social Sciences in the Management of Water Resources.* University Press of Kentucky. Lexington, Kentucky, U.S.A. 1974.

Wu, Y., and Clement, W. A. (Eds.). *Hope and Frustration.* University of Michigan, Ann Arbor, Michigan, U.S.A. 1971.

Parsons, Talcott, and Shils, Edward (Eds.). *A General Theory of Action.* Harvard University Press, Cambridge, Mass., U.S.A. 1951.

Rokeach, Milton. *Beliefs, Attitudes and Values.* Jossy-Bass Publishers, San Francisco, Calif., U.S.A. 1968.

Mei, Y. P. *Traditional Asian Values and Asian Environment.* Environment and/or Development in Asia.

Economic Development Planning Process in Developing Countries

United Nations. *Organisation and Administration of Environmental Programmes.* U.N. Publication. E.74.II.H.5.

United Nations. *Development Administration: Current Approaches and Trends in Public Administration and National Development.* U.N. Publication. E.76.II.H.1.

Land Use Planning

Twiss, Robert H. and Heyman, Ira M. *Nine Approaches to Environmental Planning.* Land Use Planning, Politics and Policy. Department of Landscape Architecture, University of California, at Berkeley, Calif., U.S.A. 1976.

International Engineering Service Consortium Pty. Ltd. *Hawkesbury River Valley Environment Investigation—Background Report. Phases I and II.* Prepared under the direction of J. G. Beale, Minister for Environment Control, New South Wales. Sydney, Australia. 1973.

Christian, C. S. and Alidrick, J. M. *Alligator River Study. Review Report of the Alligator Rivers Region environment fact-finding study.* Australian Government Publishing Service, Canberra, Australia. 1977.

Leopold, L. P., *et al. A procedure for evaluating environmental impact.* Government Printing Office, Washington, D.C., U.S.A. 1971.

Sorenson, J. *A framework for identification and control of resource degradation and conflict in the multiple use of the coastal zone.* Department of Landscape Architecture, University of California, at Berkeley, Calif., U.S.A. 1971.

Dee, N., *et al. Environment evaluation system for water resources planning.* Report to the U.S. Bureau of Reclamation, Battelle Colombus Labs., Colombus, Ohio, U.S.A. 1972.

Beale, J. G. Minister for Environmental Control. *Guidelines for Application of Environmental Impact Policy in New South Wales* (tangerine). Government Printer, Sydney, Australia. 1973.

International Council of Scientific Unions Scientific Committee on Problems of the Environment. *Environmental Impact Assessment: Principles and Procedures.* SCOPE 5. Paris. 1975.

Kozlowski, J., and Hughes, J. T. *Threshold Analysis.* Halstead Press, New York. 1972.

McHarg, Ian L. *Design with Nature.* Doubleday & Co., Inc., Garden City, New York. 1971.

Department of Ecology. *Final Guidelines, Shoreline Management Act of 1971.* State of Washington, U.S.A.

U.S. Forest Service. *Land Capabilities.* Planning Guide Map prepared for the Tahoe Regional Planning Agency. U.S.A. 1971.

Council for Scientific and Industrial Research. *South Coast Project.* Division of Land Use Research, C.S.I.R.O., Canberra, Australia. 1977.

United Nations. *Urban Land Policies and Land-Use Control Measures.* Vol. II. Asia and the Far East. U.N. Publication E.73.IV.6.

McAllister, Donald M., (Ed.). *Environment: A New Focus for Land-Use Planning.* National Science Foundation, Washington, D.C., U.S.A. 1973.

Murphy, A. H., and Winkler, R. L. *Subjective Probability Forecasting in the Real World: Some Experimental Results.* International Institute for Applied Systems Analysis (IIASA), Laxenburg, Austria. 1973.

Holling, C. S. (Ed.). *Modelling and Simulation for Environmental Impact Analysis.* International Institute for Applied Systems Analysis (IIASA), Laxenburg, Austria. 1974.

Beale, J. G. Minister for Environment Control. *Environmental Planning within the Environmental Impact Policy of the Government of New South Wales.* Sydney, Australia. 1973.

Alinsky, Saul D. *Citizen Participation and Community Organisation in Planning and Urban Renewal.* The Industrial Areas Foundation, Chicago, Illinois, U.S.A. 1962.

Pause Plan Protect. Issued Under the Authority of J. G. Beale, Minister for Environment Control, New South Wales. Sydney, Australia. 1973.

Environmental Impact Policy. Statement of Basic Principles Adopted by N.S.W. State Government. Issued under the Authority of J. G. Beale, Minister for Environment Control, New South Wales, Australia. 1973.

Turner, J. G. *South Coast Project: Summaries of Bio-Physical Background Studies.* Division of Land Use Research, Technical Memorandum 76/1. C.S.I.R.O., Canberra, Australia. 1976.

Turner, J. G. *South Coast Project: Summaries of Socio-Economic Background Studies.* Division of Land Use Research, Technical Memorandum 76/7. C.S.I.R.O., Canberra, Australia. 1976.

Austin, M. P. *South Coast Project: Generation and Appraisal of Land Use Options.* Division of Land Use Research, Technical Memorandum 76/18. C.S.I.R.O., Canberra, Australia. 1976.

Turner, J. G. *South Coast Project: Summaries of Land Function Studies.* Division of Land Use Research, Technical Memorandum 77/2. C.S.I.R.O., Canberra, Australia. 1977.

CHAPTER 13

Crucial Realities and Environmental Management

1. Links Between Population, Food and Energy

"People, people, people. Mobs, beggars. People living and dying in the streets, crammed into vehicles, herding animals. Noise, dust, smoke, filth. The stench, the heat. It was an unreal scene", said a shocked tourist from a developed country back from a first visit to a huge Asian city. Tragically, it is the reality. The picture is much the same in many cities in some less developed countries.

Planners and administrators have grappled with the problem of the adequacy of human requirements in quantitative terms. Today's need is to include a qualitative aspect as well.

While spreading over the surface of the globe, throughout the ages, many groups of human beings have succeeded in keeping their populations in harmony with their habitats. Examples, still living largely in stability with nature and their modest built environments, are some sturdy Lapps, some lethargic isolated Pacific islanders and some resilient tribes in Amazonia. They live close to nature and, in differing ways, have learnt to appreciate the tolerable limits of their surroundings. They respect natural forces and recognize the dire consequences of overloading natural resources, including excessive population pressures.

A habitat system becomes unstable where the pressures exceed the tolerable limits. Often the result has been human misery, disease, pestilence, plague, famine and death. Glen T. Seaborg* said,

---

* Glen T. Seaborg, *The Environment—and what to do about it*, Paper given at meeting of the National Academy of Sciences—National Research Council, Argonne National Laboratory, May 5, 1969, in *Nuclear News*, July 1969.

We tend to forget the extent to which nature destroys—and pollutes—segments of itself, sporadically and violently—with man often a major victim in these upheavals. Among the greatest of these were: the earthquake in Shensi Province in China in 1556, killing an estimated 800,000 people ... the volcanic eruption of 1470 B.C. that destroyed the Minoan civilisation ... the great flood of the Hwang-ho River in 1887 that swept 900,000 people to their death; the famine in India in 1770 that claimed the lives of a third of this country's population—tens of millions of people; and the 1877–78 famine in China that killed 9,500,000. And centuries before man seriously tampered with nature through modern medicine, between 1347 and 1351, the Black Death (bubonic plague) wiped out 75,000,000 people in Europe. History records numerous other types of plagues and natural disasters that have periodically destroyed various forms of life and changed the face of the earth ... long before man and his new technologies interfered with the balance of nature."

More and more people are surviving. Modern artificial life support (or death control) systems have often enabled populations to grow at rates which tend to over-extend all support systems. If this tendency proceeds too far the result is an unstable habitat and, inexorably, nature takes its toll. Man living confidently in the greater communities is sometimes shocked by nature's enormous powers.

Frequently, the mass media headline cyclones, earthquakes, tidal waves, floods, volcanic eruptions and other natural disasters. A current example of the vulnerability of developed man is the crippling 1977 blackout in New York, U.S.A., when lightning struck vital points of the huge electricity system, putting a whole city society and its institutions and morals into chaos.

In recent times, population increase and related food and energy problems have worsened. Results are seen in various degraded environments—the destruction of natural resources and the blight of city slums.

Erik P. Eckholm* vividly documents the global extent of ecological stress, its causes and consequences. He concludes:

The trends charted in this book do not point toward a sudden, cataclysmic global famine. What appears most likely, if current patterns prevail, is chronic depression conditions for the share of humankind, perhaps a fourth, that might be termed

* Erik P. Eckholm, *Losing Ground—Environmental Stress and World Food Prospects*, W. W. Norton & Company Inc., New York, 1976.

economically and politically marginal. Marginal people on marginal lands will slowly sink into the slough of hopeless poverty. Some will continue to wrest from the earth what fruits they can, others will turn up in the dead-end urban slums of Africa, Asia, and Latin America. Whether the deterioration of their prospects will be a quiet one is quite another question.

Several sources, including the United Nations Secretariat and the World Bank, estimate that the world population is now about 4 billion and will rise to about 6.3 billion by the year 2000. Robert S. McNamara, President, World Bank (address to the Massachusetts Institute of Technology, Cambridge, Massachusetts, April 28, 1977), has stated that fertility has declined in 77 of the 88 developing countries for which estimates are available. However, he concluded:

> Unless governments, through appropriate policy action, can accelerate the reduction in fertility, the global population may not stabilise below 11 billion. That would be a world none of us would want to live in.

It should be recognized that population growth is unevenly spread, and that this will tend to continue, as has been illustrated diagrammatically by Margaret R. Biswas* and reproduced here as Fig. 29.

Since the days of Malthus, developed countries particularly have pondered the subject of population increase. Most prognosis has been pessimistic. But the paradox has become more prominent—as the human race increases, its capacity to feed itself increases at a faster rate. Margaret R. Biswas and Asit K. Biswas† point out that the cereal availability *per capita*, which dominates the world food economy, increased by about 40% in 20 years, from 1951 to 1971. "Capacity" is the operative word because the capacity is not equally distributed. The reasons and the causal relationship

---

* Margaret R. Biswas, *Population, Resources and the Environment*, Resources of Southern Africa Today & Tomorrow, 1976. Proceedings of the conference held by the Associated Scientific & Technical Societies of South Africa at Johannesburg, 22–26 September 1975, The Associated Scientific & Technical Societies of South Africa, 2 Holland Street, Johannesburg 2001.

† Margaret R. Biswas and Asit K. Biswas, *Environmental Impacts of Increasing the World's Food Production*. Agriculture & Environment, 2 (291–309). Elsevier Scientific Publishing Company, Amsterdam.

The diagram indicates the population and year in each case when population
growth is expected to cease (around 2070 for Europe with a population of 698 million,
and in 2120 for Africa with 2338 million, for example)

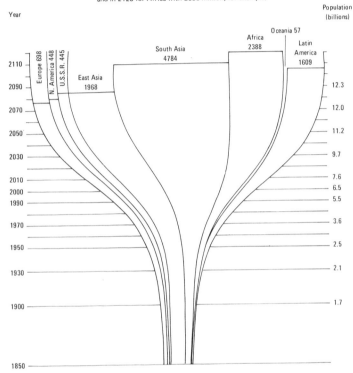

Fig. 29. Schematic Representation of the Past and Estimated Future Population of 8 Major World Regions (*from Margaret R. Biswas 1976*).

between population, food and energy supply are at the heart of the environmental dilemma. In explanation, and partly as a consequence, an improved capacity to produce food creates a demand for energy resources. Energy is needed to multiply human muscle-power in food production. More significantly, an improved level of nutrition creates a demand for creature comforts which themselves consume energy as never before.

Population increase, unmatched by the technologies to produce food efficiently and abundantly, leads to further population increases principally because submarginal farm units demand more and more undernourished human labour of decreasing work capacity. Lack of physical, mechanical and technological resources for food production leads to denuded land which in turn can only be rehabilitated by massive inputs of better technology. The improved technology does not have to be of modern industrial-society type. The replacement of shifting agriculture by hand-hewn terraced irrigation transformed the capacity of South-East Asia to feed itself many centuries ago, through intensive rice culture.

However, where the population increase has in effect "overrun" the capacity of previous technologies to expand quickly enough to maintain food supplies and living standards, there is every reason to introduce high-energy systems. In the long term, abundant food and energy, without much governmental urging, will begin to reduce rates of population increase. An expanding population assured of energy-saving methods soon realizes that fewer people are needed to ensure food production and that fewer people mean more surpluses available for individual distribution and therefore higher living standards overall.

In the medium term, governments can move, chiefly in the educational sphere, to reduce population rates of increase much sooner than long-term prosperity, which will have the same effect. Many nations have family planning programmes. Most of these, however, are inadequate to deal with the present situation, particularly in developing countries. Supporting programmes such as increasing availability of over-the-counter contraceptive products and antipregnancy methods have only slightly checked fertility rates.

Those engaged in preparing future economic and social development plans should delve more deeply into population limitation options. There is no shortage. The only limit is human ingenuity. Numerous methods of birth control are available. For ease of comparison some of the more common methods have been classified in Appendix X in a number of categories under the general headings of A. Without Contraceptives; B. Contraceptives; and C. Surgical.

There is of course wide cultural diversity in attitudes towards particular methods of contraception. No matter what values are held by the people of a nation, there are certainly means available which can be used to keep the population within the capacity of environmental support systems.

Most higher species of animals evolved complex and varied behavioural patterns to limit their numbers. It seems that primitive Man evolved such control mechanisms. V. C. Wynne-Edwards says:

> Man in the paleolithic stage, living as a hunter and gatherer, remained in balance with his natural resources just as other animals do under natural conditions. Generation after generation, his numbers underwent little or no change. Population increase was prevented not by physiological control mechanisms of the kind found in many other mammals but only by behavioural ones, taking the form of traditional customs and taboos. All Stone Age tribes that survived into modern times diminished their effective birth rate by at least one of the three ritual practices—infanticide, abortion, and abstention of intercourse. In a few cases, fertility was apparently impaired by surgery during the initiation ceremonies. In many cases, marriage was long deferred.

It should be apparent that human beings have been endowed with an organ for thinking as well as organs for reproduction. Man has ascended to higher levels of existence and organization through the use of his remarkable intelligence. Solutions to population problems can flow from the application of this intelligence.

Many in government fail to appreciate the built-in "momentum" in population increase. If fully effective family limitation were to be achieved nation-wide by tomorrow night, population would not begin to level off for at least one more generation. Over the whole length of that generation additional people have still to be fed, clothed, sheltered and educated, and with modern health programmes, sustained eventually over a much lengthened life span.

Even where current programmes have slowed population growth rates, there is still need to ensure that the rate is in keeping with the realistic development of finite physical resources. Otherwise, tomorrow's generations must suffer harshly from today's inadequate planning and management. While international aid programmes can help, the truth is that the problem is one for each individual nation to face squarely. If a nation fails to keep its numbers within tolerable limits, nature will surely do it, and probably in a way which may not be particularly humane.

It is vitally important to ensure that strategies to increase food production on a short-term basis can be sustained and effectively integrated with long-term policies. With many present policies, there is the danger that efforts to increase food production in the short run, and on a crisis basis, may lead to the adoption of strategies which are self-defeating in the long run. Any strategy to increase food production on a sustained basis that does not explicitly consider environmental factors is doomed to failure, sooner or later. Strategies must work with nature, not against it.

Within this philosophical framework, there is need to review food production variables such as food loss and wastage during production, storage and distribution; environmental constraints in relation to the use of pesticides and fertilizers; problems arising from inadequate land-use planning and irrigation practices; effects of climatic changes on food production; technology transfer and use.

It is difficult to mention energy without discussing the environment. Speak of oil drilling, and fear of oil spills is aroused. Mention coal, and air quality is a controversial topic. It is the same with wood, nuclear energy, solar energy and so on. Yet modern living standards depend greatly on having abundant energy in a variety of forms.

The energy environment can be considered in two main parts. One is concerned with the purity of air and water and the conservation of natural features. The other comprises surroundings such as homes, schools, work-places, and the economy in which society functions. The state of the economy substantially determines the affluence or poverty of daily life. And the economy depends greatly on energy. So the quality of life in today's society is also dependent on how energy is obtained and used.

Energy is required for food production, cooking, transportation, construction materials, manufacture of goods for modern society. It is needed to build roads, construct dams, erect schools, provide hospitals, power factories, replace slums. It is needed to clean air and water by removing pollutants.

It is essential to apply ecological principles in the development and use of energy sources. In the past, inadequate planning and control of mining for fuels, fuel transport, and power facilities have caused environmental deterioration. This need not be so. The change in attitude will incur cost and must come sensibly if the real interest of the people is to be served.

Governments must be prepared to delve more deeply into energy options. People will have to be prepared to tolerate some trade-offs between energy resource development and the environment in order to achieve the best result, physical, economical, and societal, for the whole community. There will be priorities to be set and a national energy policy to be established.

2. Links Between Developmental Mechanisms

Levels of population, food, and energy supplies set the realistic limits for national living standards. To achieve these in practice, however, requires the establishment and operation of development mechanisms. Applied to the realities of environmental improvement (that is, *leaving out the purely technical production aspects*) the more significant means of translating people from impoverishment to dignified living standards include:

- Physical planning
- Research
- Technology assessment
- Technology transfer
- Training, Education, Communication

Each of these is a development mechanism, closely related to its fellows.

Physical planning, in the sense of being a developmental mechanism, refers to conservation (wise use) of both natural and man-made environments and also to rehabilitation of environments destroyed by human activities. In developing countries the planned utilization of natural resources is of vital importance to accommodate the needs of expanding populations and to provide for the accelerated consumption rates of a more affluent people. Physical planning has to strike a balance between the demand for more material things and the natural resources supplying them. In striking that balance on rational grounds, it must call for supporting research, for technology transfer, and for training, education and communication services.

Research occupies a critical place among the developmental mechanisms, because it is always seen as deficient. Research workers themselves appreciate this fact, but environmental managers may not always appreciate that research is selectively deficient. Ecological linkages are rarely understood. In a derivative way, research undertaken in developed countries is used and conclusions are often suspect when transported to a different milieu. As an input to environmentally-oriented physical planning, relevant research therefore has a top priority. Without it, development will occur but it may be development which will be very expensive in the medium term.

In this regard it would be useful to list and study current environmentally oriented investigations within a nation. A format for a preliminary survey in included as Appendix XI.

Technology assessment and *technology transfer* can be inter-related in considering developmental mechanisms. Lack of applicable, or relevant research, if the lack is actually appreciated, can lead the physical planner to evaluate firstly, the importation of an already developed system and secondly, to think about transferring an already existing "package" to fill a need. Often of course the logic is reversed. An inappropriate package is sold which turns out to be incompatible with existing systems.

In many developing countries there is an opportunity to decide on alternative technologies to achieve results now obtainable from old, obsolete and inappropriate technologies in advanced countries. The opportunities for exploiting less damaging existing and new technologies should be implicit in planning environmental management systems.

The options open in many countries are not pre-empted by existing structures, systems or institutional arrangements. For example, dependence on the automobile is not always ingrained habit; greater utilization of solar energy for low-grade heat is not precluded by existing building conventions or by massive investments in fossil energy sources; agricultural use of waste process-water can often be facilitated by placing waste-water sources close to agricultural land or by planning particular production processes to utilize the water.

Exercising superior technological options depends on a whole network of decisions made by a variety of decision-makers in a variety of public and private enterprises. Technology assessment, to be carried into operation, requires an awareness that options exist and that they should be considered seriously. Co-ordinating group or administrative activities often need no more than a simple suggestion in order to place in train the sequence of decisions which act consistently to provide an environmentally superior technological system at lower social costs to the community.

Technology transfer happens continuously, and is not necessarily inadvisable. It can often solve a specific problem rapidly and economically as for example the importation of efficient well-drilling technologies to a land afflicted by drought. Where problems can occur however is where, for example, a technology primarily designed to save labour is brought uncritically to an environment in which saving labour may be detrimental to community welfare. The World Bank has recognized this over the past half-decade by encouraging rural development rather than industrialization. Most recently it has launched projects designed to finance labour-intensive small-scale industries. Such industries are not in the current advanced industrialization tradition. Transfer of traditional technologies would be counter-productive to the World Bank initiative. In fact it is possible that developing countries might eventually transfer small-scale technologies to the now "developed" world in order to assist its decentralization policies, which often lag because industries no longer have the art of adjusting to medium-scale technologies.

Training, Education and Communication is the integrating and distributive mechanism which ensures that the whole national strategy can be implemented with the entire population participating.

Related specifically to the national environmental strategy, training, education and communication should at least cover the following:

- Environmental administration
- Environmental education of children in the school system

- Environmental curricula development in universities and research establishments
- Provision of scholarships emphasizing multi-disciplinary work
- Environmental training courses—in-service, short-term, diploma, special certificate—particularly in relation to managerial and technological aspects
- Provision of reliable environmental information and briefings to the mass media
- Environmental education projects and campaigns to focus public attention on key problem areas
- Specialized programmes to alert industrial and business leaders to governmental requirements and covering environmental initiatives affecting them

Over the whole area of environmental communication there is a pressing need to present complex subjects simply and to stress linkages, both among the subject areas themselves and more especially between environmental programmes and their potential to upgrade community welfare in real and tangible ways.

So, with this background, added to the information in earlier chapters, let us consider how the environmental management process works.

Selected Bibliography

Links Between Population, Food and Energy

Seaborg, Glen T. *The Environment—and what to do about it.* Paper to a meeting at the National Academy| of Sciences. National Research Council, Argonne National Laboratory. Nuclear News. 1969.

Eckholm, Erik P. *Losing Ground: Environmental Stress and World Food Prospects.* W. W. Norton & Co., Inc., New York, U.S.A. 1976.

McNamara, Robert S. *Address to the Massachusetts Institute of Technology* (April 1977). President, World Bank, Washington, D.C.

Biswas, Margaret R. *Population, Resources and the Environment.* Resources of Southern Africa To-day and Tomorrow. The Associated Scientific and Technical Societies of South Africa, Johannesburg, Union of South Africa. 1976.

Biswas, Margaret R. and Biswas, Asit. *Environmental Impacts of Increasing the World's Food Production*. Agriculture and Environment, 2 (1975) 291–309, Elsevier Scientific Publishing Company, Amsterdam, The Netherlands.

Wood, Clive. *Contraception Explained*. World Health Organization (WHO), Geneva, Switzerland. 1975.

Department of Medical and Public Affairs. *Population Report*. The George Washington University Medical Center, Washington D.C., U.S.A.

United Nations. *Concise report on: The World Population Situation in 1970-1975 and its Long Range Implications*. U.N. Publication. E.74.XII.4.

Regional Office for Education in Asia. *Population Education in Asia: a source book*. UNESCO, Bangkok. 1975.

Division of Population and Social Commission for Asia and the Pacific. *Asian Population Programme News*. ESCAP, Thailand. 1977.

United Nations. *Report of the World Population Conference, 1974*. U.N. Publication. E.75.XIII.3.

United Nations Fund for Population Activities. *National Censuses and the United Nations*. Population Profiles 3. New York, U.S.A. 1977.

World Bank. *Population Planning: Sector Work Paper*. Washington, D.C., U.S.A. 1972.

United Nations Fund for Population Activities. *Labour and Population*. Population Profiles 5. New York. 1977.

United Nations Fund for Population Activities. *POPULI*. New York. 1977.

United Nations Fund for Population Activities. *POPULATION*. Monthly Bulletin. New York. July 1977.

International Planned Parenthood Federation. *PEOPLE*. Quarterly Bulletin. London. Vol. 4. No. 2. 1977.

World Bank. *World Bank Atlas*. Washington, D.C., U.S.A. 1976.

Wynne-Edwards, V. C. *Animal Dispersion in Relation to Social Behaviour*. Oliver and Boyd, London. 1962.

Wynne-Edwards, V. C. Science, 147 1543. 1965.

Lack, D. *The Natural Regulation of Animal Numbers*. Oxford University Press, U.K. 1954.

Calhoun, J. B., Scientific American, 206 (2) 139.

Kormondy, E. J. *Concepts of Ecology*. Prentice-Hall, New Jersey, U.S.A. 1969.

United Nations. *Asian Population Studies Series*.

    No. 2. *Family Planning, Internal Migration and\Urbanization in ECAFE Countries*. U.N. Publication. E.68.II.F.13.

    No. 3. *Report of Working Group on Communication Aspects of Family Planning Programme*. U.N. Publication. E.68.F.17.

    No. 4. *Assessment of Acceptance and Effectiveness of Family Planning Methods*. Report of an Expert Group. U.N. Publication. E.69 II.F.15.

    No. 5. *Evaluation of Family Planning Programmes*. U.N. Publication. E.69.II.F.15.

    No. 6. *Fertility Studies in the ECAFE Region*. U.N. Publication. E.72.II.F.3.

Links Between Developmental Mechanisms

Physical Planning

United Nations. *Urban Land Policies and Land-use Control Measures. Vol. II. Asia and the Far East.* U.N. Publication. E.73.IV.6.

Alonso, William. *Problems, Purposes, and Implicit Policies for a National Strategy of Urbanization.* Institute of Urban & Regional Development, University of California at Berkeley. 1971.

Alonso, William. *City Sizes and Quality of Life: Some Observations.* Institute of Urban & Regional Development, University of California at Berkeley, California, U.S.A. 1975.

Rittle, and Webber. *Dilemma in a general theory of planning.* Political Science, Vol. 4. 1973.

Meltsner, A. *Political Feasibility and Policy Analyses.* Public Administration Review, Vol. XXXII. December 1972.

Symposium on Urban Development. Convened by The National Housing Bank. Rio de Janeiro, Brazil. 1974.

Meier, Richard L. *Urban Futures Observed: in the Asian Third World.* Institute of Urban & Regional Development, University of California at Berkeley, California, U.S.A. 1976.

Research

United Nations Association of the United States of America. *Science and Technology in an Era of Independence.* A Report of a National Policy Panel. U.S.A. 1975.

Environmental Investigations 1971. Prepared under the direction of J. G. Beale, Minister for Environment Control. Sydney, N.S.W., Australia. 1972.

United Nations Environment Programme. Research Listing. UNEP, Nairobi, Kenya. 1977.

Watt, K. *Principles of Environmental Science.* McGraw Hill, New York. 1973.

Technology Assessment

National Academy of Engineering. *A Study of Technology Assessment.* Government Printing Office, Washington, D.C., U.S.A. 1969.

National Academy of Sciences and Technology. *Processes of Assessment and Choice.* Government Printing Office, Washington, D.C., U.S.A. 1969.

Coates, J. F. *Technology Assessment: The Benefits, the Costs, the Consequences.* The Futurist, Vol. 5. 1971.

Organization for Economic Co-operation and Development. *Seminar on Technology Assessment.* Directorate for Scientific Affairs, OECD, Paris. 1972.

Hetman, Francois. *Society and the Assessment of Technology.* OECD, Paris. 1973.

Technology Transfer

Cooper, C. and Sercpvotcj, F. *The Mechanism for the Transfer of Technology from Advanced to Developing Countries.* University of Sussex, U.K. 1970.

Hamilton, David. *Technology, Man and the Environment.* Faber & Faber Ltd., London. 1973.

Myrdal, G. *The Transfer of Technology to Underdeveloped Countries.* Scientific American, Vol. 231, No. 3. 1974.

Jequier, Nicholas (Ed.). *Appropriate Technology: Problems and Promises.* OECD, Paris. 1976.

Training, Education and Communication

Mathews, William H., *et al. Resource Materials for Environmental Management and Education.* The MIT Press, Cambridge, Massachusetts, U.S.A. 1976.

Swan, J. A. *Environmental Attitudes and Values and Environmental Education.* Paper to the 1st National Conference on Environmental Education. University of Wisconsin, Green Bay, Wisconsin, U.S.A. 3 December 1970.

Chow, Ven Te, *et al* (Eds.). *Water Resources Education.* Proceedings at the International Seminar on Water Resources Education. Paris. 24–29 March 1975.

Stapp, William B. *Environmental Education: a Major Advance.* Nature and Resources, Vol. XII, No. 1. Jan-March 1976.

Centre d'etudes industrielles. *International Programme in Environmental Management Education* (IPEME). Annual Report and Workshops. Conches-Geneva, Switzerland. 1977.

Glasser, Roslyn, *et al. Capabilities of Environmental Resources Education and Public Participation.* IWRA-UNESCO Education Conference, 24–25 March, 1975. UNESCO, Paris.

Connor, Desmond M. *Public Participation in Environmental Design for Public Projects.* Water Resources Publications. Fort Collins, Colorado, U.S.A. 1975.

CHAPTER 14

The Environmental Management Process

1. Cyclical Nature of Environmental Administration

"Many environmental ideas have been considered. We've tried quite a few", the administrator remarked dejectedly, "and somehow we have not been able to get it all together." This is a common observation in recent times. It draws attention to the plight of harassed administrators struggling to deal with environmental complexities—struggling often to get a coherent programme together in the face of administrative structures designed for another era.

If thoughts stray to the impossible notion of "managing the environment" the position is irretrievable. However, if it is seen clearly that the administrator's role is the intelligent management of activities within environmentally tolerable limits, then it should not be so difficult to "get it all together". The process of administration described below draws the threads together. It may not mirror any particular solution in detail, but in principle the lessons are universal.

To appreciate the cyclical nature of the administrative processes needed, it will be necessary to refer to the whole process first (see Fig. 30) and then to comment on its components (Sec. 11 of this chapter). Whole administrative "pictures" are very important—any administrator who tries to "slice the cake" will be ineffective. To some extent what follows is recapitulatory but the basics expounded are really the crux in successful attempts to upgrade deteriorating environments.

As outlined earlier, names given to functional units are descriptive

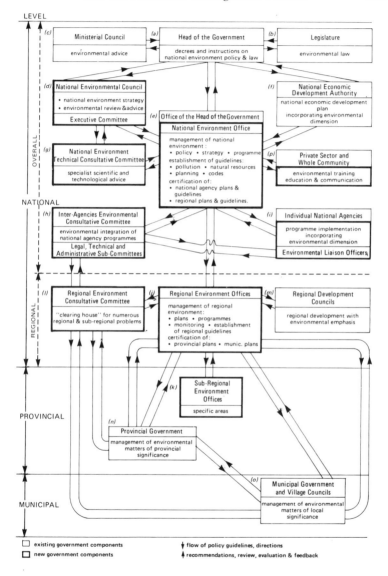

Fig. 30. Cyclical Environmental Management Process—Framework for Continuous Dialogue (*elaborated from Beale 1975*).

only. Practice and tradition will result in various names being used for the administrative units described below and in Fig. 30. Nevertheless, their counterparts will be immediately apparent to experienced professionals.

2. Environmental Content of Development

The principal objective of the whole environmental administration process is to ensure that planning and environmental aims are compatible; that conceptual areas such as pollution control, management of natural resources and environmental development planning are not confused, and that each area is supported by adequate policy, law, administration and technology.

The idea is for environmental considerations to become part and parcel of the total planning and administration process with environmental aspects being taken into account at the planning stage, and subsequently. Planning procedures must be designed to scrutinize economic, social, technical and ecological aspects in an endeavour to achieve well-balanced solutions to the problems of growth and development.

The procedures must also progressively and adequately take heed of resource capability so that development decisions automatically include environmental factors. Doing this avoids the all-too-common extensive and inefficient duplication of government agencies and private interests in planning and administration.

3. Elements of Environmental Management

The provision of the needs of modern society (*e.g.* food, clothing, energy, homes, schools, hospitals, roads, transportation, recreation, tourism) consumes resources and disturbs the environment. The aim of environmental management is to ensure intelligent management of those activities which have a significant impact on the environment. Injecting an environmental dimension into planning and administration is relevant at every stage of the management process. This generally involves the following elements:

- Identifying values
- Defining goals
- Specifying objectives
- Formulating strategies
- Choosing the appropriate strategy
- Designing the preferred programme
- Implementing the programme
- Monitoring, feedback and evaluation

Effective environmental management must also include long-range planning, early warning, speedy field reaction, quick analysis, training, education and communication.

4. Environmental Management Process

Many government agencies, numerous private organizations and a multitude of people have varying responsibilities to make plans and take actions affecting the environment. Integration of activities at all levels is necessary to ensure that well-reasoned account is taken of the likely consequences of actions throughout all sectors. As the elements listed above in Sec. 3 indicate, this is achieved if a cyclical environmental management process eventuates to provide a framework for continuous environmental dialogue. Such a system is virtually the only way to ensure constant review and updating to meet dynamic environmental challenges.

5. Responsibilities at Various Government Levels

In Chap. 6, Governmental Systems, institutional arrangements to integrate governmental actions were discussed. It is critical to recognize the responsibilities and functions of various governmental levels in looking at environmental management as a cyclic process.

(*a*) *National level.* To be fully effective an environmental management system needs a strong legal base. National law should provide support for broadly-based national policies to guide pollution control, management of natural resources and environmental planning at all governmental levels. The law must be binding on government agencies and, through the government decision-making role, on private organizations and individuals.

(b) *Regional Level.* National law should institute at the regional level the assessment of resources, their capabilities and anticipated effects of proposed development. This must be the legal basis for regional planning, resource management and pollution control guidelines. Resource capabilities need to be certified as being within prescribed national policies and guidelines.

(c) *Subregional level.* National law should institute at provincial, municipal, local and other subregional levels the management of environmental matters of subregional significance. Actions taken must be certified as being within prescribed regional guidelines.

6. Economic, Social and Technical Content

Economic, social and technical components are integral parts of the management process. Economic objectives should take account of equity, the economic feasibility of development proposals, and the social cost to the community rather than sheer economic cost efficiency. Social objectives should promote the well-being of people and the quality of life. Technology assessment is necessary to ensure that the best available options are utilized to make environmental progress a reality.

Common to all levels of the environmental management process is the need for clear statements on:

(a) basic economic, social and technical objectives of proposals;

(b) assumptions made to achieve those objectives, including the extent to which public views have been sought and taken into account;

(c) likely consequences of specific proposals on various community groups; and

(d) likely impacts of programmes on the environment.

7. Public Participation

Advantages can often be gained from public participation in development and this can be encouraged through:

(*a*) availability to the public of full information (in easily understood form) from the earliest planning stage;

(*b*) adequate opportunity for people to contribute ideas at all stages in the planning process;

(*c*) opportunity for public response to influence plans (there can be much more wisdom in earthy, unsophisticated advice);

(*d*) care being taken to ensure that a strong sectional interest does not become the total "public interest" due to the timidity or apathy of the general community.

(*e*) time limits for public contributions to avoid unnecessary delays and procrastination.

8. Government Agency Participation

Clearly, as seen in earlier chapters, it is essential for government agencies at all levels to be involved in, and committed to, the environmental management process. Too often there is a tendency for the local representatives of national agencies to lack power to speak authoritatively (or at all) on their agency's plans. Sometimes this causes uncertainty and confusion at lower government levels. It always slows decisions throughout the entire administrative system.

There is also a tendency for national agencies to ignore regional, subregional, and public views in formulating policies and plans. Primarily this results in insufficient knowledge and understanding of the issues at stake.

Government agencies at all levels should be committed to, and involved in, the environmental management process through a framework for continuous dialogue incorporating:

(*a*) inter-agency consultation and co-ordination;

(*b*) national officials participating in regional and subregional discussions;

(*c*) these officers having sufficient autonomy to commit their agencies so as to avoid unnecessary referral to their head offices; and

(*d*) national agencies having environmental focal points within their administration.

9. National Environmental Development Planning

From the discussion in Chapter 12, Environmental Planning, it will be noted that an essential goal of environmental development planning is to provide a basis upon which the most effective development strategy (a mixture of economic, social and technical development aims with conservation concepts) can be formulated. The results of some of the recent growth strategies in many nations indicate a lack of appreciation of the real economic, technical and social and environmental consequences in decision making. There are, unfortunately, too many examples of ineffective use of resources, inefficient investment policies and the pursuit of priorities resulting in environmental degradation.

Planning techniques have been developed in many advanced countries in an attempt to deal with the historic tendency for rapid growth to occur by rural migration into congested, polluted and slum-fringed cities while the rest of the country declines. Many of the techniques, however, are still experimental and success has been sporadic. (Refer to Chap. 12.)

Planning practices differ considerably between countries just as do their individual, political, legislative, economic and social systems. Results from the application of these practices have varied so greatly that the imposition in full measure of any particular system of regional planning formulated in a developed country is unlikely to prove entirely successful in developing countries. Yet the loose transfer of international technology occurs repeatedly, often with deleterious effects as outlined in Chap. 13.

It is necessary to assess conditions within a developing country relative to those of the country providing the model in order to find a basis for initiating new planning approaches. It can be noted that effective planning practices in developed countries have been supported generally by a strong existing legislative base, administrative experience at all levels of government, qualified and experienced planning professionals, and finance. While any system should take into account international knowledge, particularly where techniques have been tested in developing countries, it must be based on a realistic view of the local situation to ensure effective results.

Most countries which were primarily agricultural and are now experiencing rapid population and industrial growth, lack depth in managerial and professional skills. Qualifications and experience show a tendency to grade downward sharply within lower echelons of government. The legislative base is usually weak or exists without any provision for effective enforcement. Doubtless in time these deficiencies will be corrected through legislation, education and experience. In the meantime, however, they must be considered as constraints which necessitate adoption initially of a practical planning system including simple procedures and codes which ensure that environmental hazards are minimized.

There is usually a need for centralized control of national environmental guidelines. However, there should be some decentralization for the design of regional guidelines. There is need also for decentralized action at the regional and local levels without the necessity for referral to national authority provided this action is within the limits of these guidelines.

10. Environmental Development Plans

As will be seen from earlier chapters, plans should be of three basic types:

(a) national policies (sometimes expressed through guidelines);
(b) regional strategies (sometimes expressed through subregional structure plans); and

(c) subregional plans (which could deal with local structure or detailed zonings and development control regulations for the whole or part of a local area). (Refer also to Chap. 13, Physical Planning.)

All plans should be set out: planning objectives, assumptions, data, alternatives considered, justification for (and implications of) the chosen course of action, regulations and specifications of the actual plan, and steps taken towards public participation in the process. They should be accompanied by maps and diagrams to illustrate intent. The plan should be expressed in non-technical, non-legal, easy-to-understand (but specific) terms free of jargon, with emphasis on the primary plan objective.

11. Framework for Continuous Dialogue—Fig. 30.

a. Need for Continuous Dialogue

To deal effectively with ever-changing circumstances, an environmental management system needs to be flexible and to ensure continuous and efficient dialogue between governments, governmental agencies, the private sector and the community at large. The important elements of a possible framework to achieve continuous dialogue are shown in Fig. 30, in which the downward arrows indicate the flow of policies, guidelines and directions. The upward arrows indicate the flow of recommendations for approval, reviews, evaluations and feedback of information.

It should be noted that the Head of the Government (a) plays the primary role, since he is in contact with the National Assembly (b) and is advised by his Cabinet (c).

b. National Environment Council

A National Environment Council (d) preferably should be chaired by the Head of the Government. Representation should include a small number of appropriate Secretaries of State (Cabinet rank) *e.g.* health, agriculture, industry, public works, transport, natural resources, and a Secretary-General. The Council would be required to elaborate and review national environment strategies continuously for the whole of the nation.

c. National Environment Office

A National Environment Office (*e*) preferably should be within the jurisdiction of the Head of the Government. The head of this office should also be Secretary-General of the National Environment Council.

The office should have the responsibility, under the direction of the Head of the Government for National Environmental Management for supervisory, advisory and co-ordinating functions, relating to pollution control, management of natural resources and environmental planning.

It is essential to establish continuous, prompt and effective dialogue between the Head of the Government (*a*) and the Council (*c*), between the Head of the Government (*a*) and the Office (*e*), between the Council (*c*) and the Office (*e*), between the Office and the National Economic and Social Development Authority (*f*), so that policies quickly respond to current needs and always have adequate legal, fiscal, administrative and technical backing to achieve national environmental objectives compatible with other national objectives.

In addition to the preparation of submission for formulation and implementation of national environment strategies, this Office (*e*) should prepare national guidelines in key functional areas such as Environmental Planning, Environmental Impact Assessment, Management of Resources (renewable and non-renewable) and Pollution Control.

National guidelines must be legally binding on all government organizations at all levels, and through their decision-making roles on the private sector, including individuals. The office would also need to have specific power and responsibility to certify that actions at all government levels (including national agencies) comply with these guidelines.

The National Environment Office (*e*) should be assisted as necessary by a team consisting of disciplinarians (experts in a particular field), multi-disciplinarians (experts in two or more fields), and inter-disciplinarians (generalists) in academic, planning and administration fields. This team should be capable of taking broad, intelligent policy approaches to complex environmental problems. These could be drawn from specialist agencies and other sources as required or otherwise attached to the Office, the form depending on the type of Office preferred by the Government.

It should be the responsibility of the Office to establish and maintain an effective dialogue with the public and private sectors and the whole community through an environmental training, education and communication programme as discussed in Chap. 13.

d. *National Environment Technical Consultative Committee*

It is essential that the Government is provided with information based on well-balanced scientific and technological advice of high quality. It would seem that the best way to achieve this would be by creating a highest level multi-disciplinary National Environment Technical Consultative Committee (*g*) comprising academics, consultants and government officials. Its charter would be to provide independent specialist advice to the Head of the Government, the Council and the Office.

e. *Inter-Agencies Environmental Consultative Committee*

Separate from the general preparation and implementation of the National Environment Strategy, there will be need for national level inter-organization discussions to minimize the effects of the usual independent and fragmented approaches of individual agencies. This integration might be accomplished through regular meetings at an Inter-Agencies Environmental Consultative Committee (*h*) whose membership should comprise the Heads of National Agencies (*i*) or their representatives. Meetings should be convened by a representative of the Head of the Government.

Undoubtedly, this Committee would benefit from the support of Legal, Technical and Administrative Subcommittees appointed to provide continuous specialized advice in these fields.

In order to implement effectively the Inter-Agency component of environmental management, it is essential to ensure that individual agencies have the best possible knowledge and understanding of governmental strategies and programmes. The effectiveness of the total government effort can be increased by the nomination of specific focal points such as environmental officers or, where more appropriate, environmental committees within individual agencies.

f. Regional Environment Offices

The role of the National Government at the regional level is management of decision making relating specifically to the regional environment. Legal instruments should provide for environmental planning in specific regions through Regional Environment Offices (*j*). They would need to work in close association with any existing regional bodies.

These Regional Offices could be small branches of the National Environment Office. They should be staffed with professional personnel capable of producing detailed regional guidelines within the limits of national policies and guidelines. Initially they could be small units within an existing body.

It is at this level that initiatives need to be taken to produce information in a suitable form (e.g. background report, reviews, inventories) for planners and decision makers, and to make the studies required for the preparation of regional guidelines. Regional Offices need authority to certify that plans prepared by agencies within their respective areas comply with the regional guidelines. They also need to lay down the avenues for public information and participation.

g. Subregional Environment Offices

In some areas, when a heavy concentration of effort is required, it may be necessary to establish Subregional Environment Offices (*k*). These should be branches of the Regional Office and generally give specific emphasis to special environmental programmes.

h. Regional Groupings

It is desirable to have a flexible approach to regional groupings. Some may need to have a "task force" concentration; in some cases it may be better to take a broad general approach. There can be advantages in using the "city-state" concept, for example, national metropolitan complexes with unique problems might be created as regions in their own right. In this event, there would probably be need for co-ordinated subregional planning within the metropolis.

i. Regional Environment Consultative Committees

There will be many problems which are of concern to all governmental levels, and which can be resolved through suitable discussions at regional level without clogging the administrative machinery. It would seem best for this effort to take place at meetings of Regional Environment Consultative Committees (*l*). Membership of the Committee should generally comprise the senior representatives of appropriate national agencies in the region. Additionally, there should be a leavening of representation from appropriate Provinces and Municipalities within the region.

It is important that national agency representation should be at sufficient levels of competence and authority to avoid unnecessary and often cumbersome referral to higher levels on matters within a region. It is essential that this Consultative Committee should be a "clearing house" mixing "downwards" policy, guidelines and directions with "upwards" recommendations, information and aspirations.

j. Regional Development Councils

Often Regional Development Councils (*m*) and similar bodies are established to perform useful functions in their several regions.

Where they exist, it is essential for the Regional Environment Offices to promote continuous dialogue with them.

k. Provincial Government

Provincial Governments (*n*) usually have important roles defined by the constitution. It is essential that as much as possible of their decentralized powers and responsibilities be used fully in implementing the national environment strategy. It is essential to ensure that steps are taken to promote the generation of sound environmental attitudes at this level, for example, through training and education programmes.

Provinces have an important place in the framework for continuous dialogue. They should be involved in several ways, first, by acting within their own powers and responsibilities on the management of environmental matters of Provincial significance within the limits of nationally approved regional guidelines; secondly, by regional groupings to achieve regional environmental objectives within the scope of national and regional guidelines; thirdly, by co-operating in special national environment enhancement programmes; fourthly, by working closely with the municipalities and other localized forms of government (*e.g.* village councils).

l. Local Government

Municipal Government (*o*) is often a "primary political unit", with considerable autonomy within the national governmental system. Municipality, town and village can play important roles in any national programme to enhance the environment. Their primary areas of responsibility are to manage environmental matters of local significance within the limits of national and regional guidelines.

In total, local governments may have decentralized powers and responsibilities in many matters pertaining to local life such as urbanization, supplies, circulation, culture, sanitation, social assistance, credit, popular institutes, tourism and police. As far as practicable, their involvement in the national plan should be encouraged. Initially, however, in order to make best use of limited resources, it would seem prudent to concentrate efforts on those with the most urgent problems. The involvement can be widened progressively as resources become available.

The first step towards involving municipalities and towns should be the promulgation of national guidelines (overall and regional) under appropriate legislation and through regulations on national environmental standards. In these matters national powers should be binding on all levels of government, on the private sector, and on individuals.

It must be emphasized that far too often an important deficiency in the expressed national intentions to enhance the environment is lack of national guidelines to assist governments at other levels. Another common deficiency is the lack of information flowing from the lower levels into higher levels of governmental administration. Directive mechanisms are usually needed to ensure meaningful and continuous dialogue.

Development (including demolition) control will generally be the responsibility of local government. Appropriate guidelines should substantially reduce the volume of referrals to higher authority and greatly assist local citizens to gain prompt decisions.

12. Special procedures

Special procedures, applicable to various governmental levels, will be required to make the proposed framework operate inter-governmentally.

The National Environment Office should provide a series of planning aids ranging from simple check-lists to sophisticated protocol depending on level of government. For example:

- Simple check-lists (in non-technical language) for use in minor environmental matters (a simple declaration of environmental factors)
- Simple interaction charts (as the basis for simple environmental impact statements) for use on slightly more complicated matters
- Simple codes (*e.g.* simple building regulations)

- Flow charts (cause—condition—effect) as the basis for environmental impact assessment
- Environmental impact assessment guidelines for matters of major environmental significance
- Formats for preparation of inventories, identification of constraints, and other aspects of environmental development planning
- Formats for planning procedures based on appropriate international techniques
- Guide to complete planning approaches (developed over a reasonable period of time as a result of experience)
- Briefings to the diplomatic service for use in international discussions on the environment, resource development, etc.

13. Training of Personnel

There will be need at all governmental levels to train personnel in practical environmental administration and procedures. Some of this could be in-service training conducted by national specialists. It should be related to the general environmental education programmes and appropriate specialized activities outlined in Chap. 13.

14. Monitoring

There is nearly always need to institute regular monitoring of the progress being made at all governmental levels. This should be directed at evaluating management systems promoting co-ordination in achieving national goals, ensuring compliance with national policies, evaluating and incorporating validated information for future programmes. Initially this could be done through the assignment of existing decentralized personnel (*e.g.* foresters, medical officers). Later, the overall position could be improved by the National Environment Office taking the initiative by arranging for special teams to brief governmental organizations on environmental objectives.

15. Enforcement

There is generally need for penalties for breaches of plans and unauthorized development (including the destruction of historic sites), and for firm enforcement of the laws and regulations. However, to be effective, the sanction imposed needs to be a reasonable balance between coercion and co-operation. It is often much more effective in real terms to impose a "stop work until made good" order on a developer, than to impose a monetary fine, which will be passed to the whole community as an increased "cost of operation".

16. Appeals and Disputes

An environmental management system needs adequate provision to deal with appeals and disputes, including third-party appeals against approvals by governments. To avoid unnecessary procrastination there should be specific time limits for submitting and hearing appeals. In many cases the appeals could be held in an informal atmosphere with the object of achieving sensible solutions. Consideration might be given to the employment of public advocate planners to assist both appellants and the appellate body in particularly technical situations.

Environmental management systems should try to ensure that appeals and disputes procedures concentrate on the substance of the issue and not on the legal precedents. If legality is allowed to intrude unduly it always overwhelms the real environmental issue.

17. Compensation

There will usually be need for compulsory acquisition of property or land for essential public purposes. For unoccupied land, this might be at the unrestricted current market value, or occupied land, perhaps the cost of re-establishment in equal circumstances in the locality or compensation for disturbance. Consideration might also be given to how excessive "windfalls" arising from public rezoning proposals should be taxed to some degree.

Commercially obsolete buildings of cultural or aesthetic value (national heritage) are in a special category. Compensation procedures need to be innovating and flexible, utilizing such financial devices as lease-backs, relief from taxation, subsidization of uneconomic uses consistent with their character and so on.

18. Roles of Planners and Managers

Incorporation of the roles of planners and environmental managers into a coherent system pose problems.

Past planning failures in many countries have resulted from planners and decision makers adopting master-type plans which have taken planners such a long time to prepare that they prove to be obsolete on implementation. Often these have been merely physical land-use plans turned into words. (Refer to Chaps. 12 and 13.)

Environmental development planning must be seen as a continuous management process in which planners provide decision makers with a range of options in response to policy directives. The information must be in a readily understood form to assist in achieving practical short-term solutions while leaving options open to meet foreseeable future situations.

Actually to make decisions (as has been pointed out in Chap. 12), managers must avoid getting "bogged down" in detail—experts tend to be immersed in detail. Managers must actively seek out a wide variety of alternatives—experts tend to concentrate on the expert advice of associates. Managers do not need a mass of information on physical plans in technical jargon. What they need is a "brief" in simple (but precise) terms, incorporating a comprehensive range of information on investment, institutional activities, essential services, environment, people, with advice on what the options entail. In this way they can make decisions promptly and consistently.

19. Availability of Data

More research is always needed for tomorrow, but there is even greater need for the inflow of today's data (including current research and investigation results) into today's environmental management process. While a data bank of reliable information is being built up, always costly and time consuming, the opportunity should be taken to assess currently available information and collate it in the form of background reports, reviews and inventories. From this should flow the primary identification of conflicts and constraints, the solution of immediate problems and the identification of areas requiring further investigation and research. Material of this nature is also essential to the procedures including monitoring which are mentioned above. (Chap. 12.)

So much for the environmental management process, now to see how a government can get action started.

Selected Bibliography

Beale, J. G. *Environmental Development Planning System.* Elizabeth Bay, N.S.W., Australia. 1975.

CHAPTER 15

Action Plans

At this stage it is often the practice to introduce case studies related to individual environmental management situations. To do this is to fail to get the message. My purpose in the preceding pages has been to encourage a "total environment" approach to management and administration and in so doing to concentrate on the practicalities rather than the more esoteric aspects of theory and philosophy. It may be useful, however, to give an idea of the elements of an *Action Plan*, as mentioned in Chap. 9, designed to make things happen within a comprehensive environmental policy.

Consider a mythical developing nation. Let us say it is primarily an agricultural country with a plantation-type commodity economy welded to subsistence farming together with a small but growing industrial sector. Exports are essentially natural resources commodities. Let us also say that the population is increasing rapidly, tourism is developing quickly and there are trends towards major urbanization. There is crowding, there are slums, there is poverty, and levels of technology in the agricultural sector are good in the plantations but poor among farmers.

There would of course be visible signs of environmental deterioration, primarily the results of certain degrading agricultural, pastoral and forestry techniques, mining, foreshore erosion, marine resource destruction and crowding around established city fringes.

The amount of industrial pollution would not be very large at this stage although there would be some serious localized incidents. While environmental deterioration is less than in most developed countries there are already signs of most types of environmental problems. Soundly-based environmental initiatives taken immediately would be needed to forestall possible future crises.

Let us say also that the existing legal and administrative structures relating to the environment, first implemented in the colonial era, with later *ad hoc* amendments and innovation, are scattered and lack co-ordination. The infrastructure is obviously inadequate to cope with current problems. These problems have been aggravated in recent years by growing industrialization, food and fuel shortages, the population explosion, tourism and the increased exploitation of natural resources.

Let us study this "case" against the systems proposed earlier in this book. An *Action Plan* should come out as a *staged* programme which might look something like the following:

Action Plan

Partly as a result of its contact with international agencies, partly as the result of pressures from its emerging populist elite, our mythical developing nation decides to do something about the "environment". What? Aided by international agencies, to which it subscribes, it enlists their aid to ultimately receive a report.

This Environmental Investigation Report indicates that changes in institutional arrangements and other actions are required to ensure effective environmental management without crippling its efforts to develop. The necessary far-reaching policy, law and administrative changes obviously cannot all occur at once. Therefore, the government needs to determine the pace appropriate to its interests, resources and commitments, commensurate with the attitude of the whole community. The Report has probably given the outline of an Action Plan for consideration by the government should it decide to proceed with initiatives along the lines of those recommended.

1. First Priorities for Action

- Set up a Ministerial Subcommittee on the Environment, presided over by the Head of the Government, other members being appropriate ministers, *e.g.* Economic Planning, Health, Agriculture, Secondary Industry. (Later, consideration could be given to expanding this Ministerial Committee into a National Environmental Council by including members from inside and outside government.)

- Establish a National Environment Office, within the administration of the Head of the Government, to service the National Environment Council. Appoint a Director-General for the Environment to be head of the Office, and to serve *ex-officio* as secretary of the National Council.

- Set up, within the National Environment Office, necessary professional units, principally Environmental Planning, Natural Resources Management, Pollution Control and Monitoring. This staff needs to be well qualified in their own specialities and also be competent generalists (technical administrators) able to cope with problems through a multi-disciplinary approach.

- Set up an Inter-Agency Environmental Consultative Committee presided over by the Director-General for the Environment, other members being the heads of those National Agencies which carry out activities of environmental significance. This Committee should be supported by Legal, Technical and Administrative Sub Committees, to assist in making recommendations for streamlining governmental administration in these areas.

- Establish a National Environmental Technical Consultative Committee comprising a multi-disciplinary group of distinguished scientists and technologists drawn from governmental, academic and private fields.

- Commence enactment of necessary legislation: Comprehensive law, specific laws (air, water, noise), amendments to existing laws.

2. Second Priorities for Action

- Appoint Regional Environment Officers to work in co-operation with regional development councils. (Initially an existing official

in a region might be assigned to look into environmental problems, and he could probably be serviced by his normal agency.)

- Establish "clearing-house"-type Regional Environment Consultative Committees presided over by Regional Environment
  Officers, other members being senior officials from the various
  national agencies serving in the region and other regional bodies
  together with several experienced people drawn from the local
  government tier. They should be serviced by the staff of the
  Regional Environment Offices.
- Set up a small Environment Unit in the National Economic
  and Social Development Planning Authority to liaise with the
  National Environment Office. (Initially personnel might be drawn
  from suitable existing officials within the Authority or, alterna-
  tively, personnel could be seconded from other departments, part-
  time or full-time.)

3. Third Priorities for Action

- Appoint Subregional Environment Officers where there is need
  for special concentration on a particular geographic area (municipality, city-state) or on solving the problems facing particular
  local government administrations.
- Encourage the appointment of Environment Liaison Officers
  within local government bodies which are experiencing significant
  environmental problems.
- Establish from time to time a number of specialist working
  parties (*e.g.* air, water, noise, waste, energy, resources, planning)
  to provide expert inputs to the relevant components of government, to aid the solution of pressing environmental problems.
  Ensure that these groups have a finite life. Failure to arrange for
  their demise leads them otherwise to continue manufacturing
  problems.

4. Development of an Interim Organization

It is obvious that to complete the above actions would require
careful planning and commitment of resources such as money, facilities, special skills. However, it is important to recognize that there

need not necessarily be, in total, an expanded bureaucracy. What is required is a redistribution of existing personnel and resources, and special training of those engaged in environmentally oriented activities to ensure more efficient injection of an environmental dimension at every decision-making stage. The achievement of a practical programme is certainly within the capability of the governments of developing countries. Success will depend greatly on the practical capacity of these administrators handed the environmental "hot potato" by their governmental masters.

Pending the implementation of governmental actions necessary to get a National Environment strategy fully operational it is usually a practical move for the Government to establish an interim organization authorized to undertake preparatory organizational work. Initially it should concentrate on designing the structure of the proposed new components of government and on restructuring other components of government so as to implement a national environment strategy at all governmental levels with outreach to the private sector and the whole community.

Next it might draft the first broad national environmental guidelines and any necessary legislation. Initially experienced administrative personnel might be obtained, part-time or full-time, by secondment from appropriate specialist departments and semi-official bodies such as national science Academies or councils. The interim organization should be headed by a distinguished leader technically knowledgeable in environmental matters and also experienced in administration.

While awaiting enactment of necessary legislation, by administrative action, the Government should direct all agencies and other governmental bodies to ensure that, before taking any actions which may have significant impact on the environment, they consider carefully the likely consequences of development, taking steps to ensure that there is minimal environmental deterioration in every case. The private sector and the community must of course be bound in this through the decision-making role of government (*e.g.* licensing, registration, permits, etc).

5. *Moving to Forestall Crises*

Action Plans must be anticipatory. Crisis areas can be foreseen but not always can the exact shape of the crisis. Most governments have already taken certain actions towards anticipating those crises denying a better quality of life for their peoples. Most countries are in a position to reduce environmental deterioration and to enhance their environments, but achieving this is never easy. It should be recognized, however, that there are plenty of examples of serious environmental problems and that comprehensive initiatives need to be taken now to forestall future environmental crises.

There are many options available to the Government and consideration should be given to the local design of intelligent "mythical" developing country approaches to meet internal environmental challenges and regional and global environmental commitments.

CHAPTER 16

Concluding Remarks

"Within the United Nations Environment Programme there is practical and realistic belief in the ability of Man to solve his environmental problems and protect his environment, while at the same time achieving a sustainable level of development that will not damage the finite resources of our earth", said Dr. Mostafa K. Tolba, in his speech to the U.N. Economic and Social Council, in July 1976.

Whether or not one believes Doomsday is imminent is a matter for personal judgement. More than 99% of the world's population reflect the primacy of the survival instinct in man by rejecting the possibility. The thesis in this book rests with the majority. There is widespread environmental degradation, and there will be more, but Doomsday is obviously not here and can be postponed indefinitely by intelligent management of our environment.

Accepting this prognosis one is left with the problem of diagnosing those trends which could bring Doomsday closer. The world is faced with controlling pollution, managing resources conservatively with long-term objectives in view and introducing environmental planning. This will not happen by accident.

The nations of the world share only one earthly environment. Among themselves and individually they will need to prescribe measures to protect and enhance the environment. This also will not happen fortuitously.

A central proposition in this book is that institution-building is a key element in the environmental management process. This involves a total international and national commitment to the environment viewed in its totality and, flowing from this, legislative, administrative and technical structures which can in fact implement national environmental strategies. The national effort must commit governments at all levels, the private sector and the community at large.

Institutions which are not designed with the above objectives in view will bring Doomsday closer rather than delaying its arrival indefinitely. The bureaucrats and administrators therefore bear a heavy burden—without their skills the best political wills in the world can be to no avail.

Most important, no nation should feel that it has to wait for foreign experts, international agencies, international agreements or outside financial aid before taking action. There are numerous opportunities to be self-reliant. The basic rules are few and the basic object in the preceding chapters has been to lay them out for administrators free of frills.

Constructive actions will forestall crises, but the choice of options will not be easy. The safe course will often be unpopular, a challenge which decision makers should tackle in the right spirit. Achieving sound environmental goals is satisfaction in itself.

A competent administrator who "sees dimly at a distance, but *does* what lies at hand" will always make things happen within environmentally tolerable limits.

Epilogue

In the *Epilogue and Apologue to Calculus Made Easy*, first published in 1910, Silvanus P. Thompson confidently assumed that when his book fell into the hands of professional mathematicians they would "damn it as being a thoroughly bad book". There was some criticism but, as years went by, increasing numbers of engineers attested to its invaluable assistance in setting them on the right track.

Some people will undoubtedly claim that *The Manager and the Environment* isn't a good book. In their view it probably makes the grievous errors of taking a simple view of a highly complex subject and of making numerous aspects of "environmental management" seem easy. In practice, however, the simple way is often successful.

Others might assert it gives away trade secrets. So it does. By illustrating "what one fool can do, another can" it shows that many who pride themselves overly on mastery of complex environmental fields, have no great reason for "ego tripping".

There are those who might allege it fails to demonstrate its methods to readers with rigid scientific logic. True enough. But, should the operation of a car be denied to someone who can't make one?

Some might claim it leaves out some difficult things. True. In fact that is the reason for writing the book. It is directed at administrators and other decision makers who have been discouraged from acquiring the elements of "environmental management" by the sheer mass of turgid academic prose. Any subject can be made repulsive by presenting it overloaded with difficulties. My objective has been to help beginners in environmental management to learn its meaning, acquire familiarity with its scope and grasp its methods of solving problems. All of this without being compelled to toil through complicated and often irrelevant academic gymnastics, so dear to many unpractical people.

People who say the approaches in the book "might be all right in practice but won't work out in theory" have of course answered themselves.

The aim has been to arrive at the frontiers of environmental problem solving. Orientation has been provided for practical environmental initiatives. May you have the satisfaction of making environmental improvement happen within your own area of work.

Appendices

ENVIRONMENTAL LAW AND ADMINISTRATION
(Format for preliminary survey)

	General	Pollution control						Natural resources management						Environmental planning						Procedures		
		Water	Air	Waste	Noise	Visual	Research	Soil	Water	Forest	Land	Marine	Research	Economic	Social	Education	Preservation	Conservation	Research	Licensing	Penalties	Appeals
Law																						
Administration																						

APPENDIX II

GOVERNMENTAL AGENCIES ADMINISTERING ENVIRONMENTAL LAW
(*Format for preliminary survey*)

TABLE 1

Key to abbreviations used in the tabulation

Agency	Abbreviation

TABLE 2

The list below identifies the environmental law within the jurisdictions of governmental agencies. Agencies have been tabulated against their areas of responsibility and environmental laws

Areas of responsibility	Relevant laws	Jurisdiction
Pollution control measures in general		
Air pollution		
Water pollution		
Waste disposal		
Noise pollution		
Noxious trades		
Pollution by radioactivity		
Agriculture		
Conservation of nature		
Pollution of soil		
Visual pollution		
Environmental planning		
Other		

APPENDIX III

**ENVIRONMENTAL EXPERTISE AVAILABLE WITHIN
GOVERNMENTAL AGENCIES**
(*Format for preliminary survey*)

TABLE 1

Key to abbreviations used in the tabulation

Agency	Abbreviation

TABLE 2

The list below identifies the expertise available within government agencies. Agencies have been tabulated against characteristics and conditions of the environment.

Characteristics and conditions	Agency

1. Physical and chemical characteristics
    Earth
        Mineral resources
        Construction material
        Soils
        Land form
        Force fields and background radiation
        Unique physical features
    Water
        Surface
        Ocean
        Underground
        Quality
        Temperature
        Recharge
        Snow and ice

Characteristics and conditions	Agency

    Atmosphere
        Quality (gases, particulates)
        Climate (Micro, Macro)
        Temperature
    Processes
        Floods
        Erosion
        Deposition (Sedimentation, Precipitation)
        Solution
        Sorption (ion exchange, complexing)
        Compaction and settling
        Stability (Slides, Slumps)
        Stress-strain (Earthquake)
        Air Movements
2. Biological conditions
    Flora
        Trees
        Shrubs
        Grass
        Crops
        Microflora
        Aquatic plants
        Endangered species
        Barriers
        Corridors
    Fauna
        Birds
        Land animals including reptiles
        Fish and shellfish
        Benthic organisms
        Insects
        Microfauna
        Endangered species and unique areas
        Barriers, Natural and artificial
        Corridors
3. Cultural factors
    Land use
        Wilderness and open spaces
        Wetlands
        Forestry
        Grazing
        Agriculture

Appendix III, Table 2 (*contd.*)

Characteristics and conditions	Agency

     Residential
     Commercial
     Industrial
     Mining and quarrying
   Recreation
     Hunting
     Fishing
     Boating
     Swimming
     Camping and hiking, sporting
     Picnicking
     Resorts
   Aesthetics and human interest
     Scenic views and vistas
     Wilderness qualities
     Open space qualities
     Landscape design
     Unique physical features
     Parks and reserves
     Monuments
     Rare and unique species or ecosystems
     Historical or archaeological sites and objects
     Presence of misfits
   Cultural status
     Cultural patterns (life style)
     Health and safety
     Employment
     Population density
   Man-made facilities and activities
     Structures
     Transportation network (movement access)
     Utility networks
     Waste disposal
     Barriers
     Corridors
4. Ecological relationships
     Salinization of water resources
     Eutrophication
     Disease-insect vectors
     Food chains
     Salinization of surficial material
     Brush encroachment
     Other

POTENTIAL POLLUTION PROBLEMS
(Format for preliminary survey)

Name (industry, or project, or system, or action, etc) ....

Pollutant	Information required					
	Type	Amounts	Sources	Monitoring systems	Control systems	Management and maintenance routines for pollution control
Liquid effluents						
Gaseous or particulate emissions						
Solid wastes						
Noise						

APPENDIX V

CHECK-LIST OF AREAS OF HUMAN CONCERN UNDER ENVIRONMENTAL
IMPACT

A check-list for deciding the areas of human concern that may be affected by
activities which cause environmental impact

1. Economic and occupational status

    Population displacement; population relocation for employment opportunities;
    services and distribution patterns; income; property values

2. Social pattern or life style

    Resettlement; rural depopulation; population density change; food; housing;
    goods; nomadic; settled; pastoral; agricultural; rural; industrial; urban; tourist

3. Social amenities and relationships

    Family life styles; schools; transportation; community feelings; participation
    or alienation; local and national pride or regret; stability; disruptions; language;
    hospitals; clubs; active and passive recreation; neighbourliness or hostility;
    assimilation or discrimination

4. Psychological features

    Involvement; expectations; stress; frustrations; commitment; challenges; work
    satisfaction; national and community pride; freedom of choice; stability and
    continuity; self-expression; company or solitude; mobility

5. Physical amenities (intellectual, cultural and aesthetic)

    Heritage; wildlife; national parks; art galleries and museums; concert halls;
    historic and archaeological monuments; landscape; wilderness; quiet; clean air,
    water and land

6. Health

    Changes in health; medical services; medical standards; public hygiene

7. Personal security

    Freedom from molestation; freedom from natural disasters

8. Religion and traditional belief

    Symbols; taboos; customs; values; freedom

9. Technology

    Security; hazards; safety measures; benefits; waste emissions; congestion; density

10. Cultural

    Leisure; fashion and clothing changes; new values; heritage; traditional and
    religious rites

11. Aesthetic

    Visual physical changes; moral conduct; traditional and sentimental values

12. Political

    Authority; level and degree of involvement; priorities; decision-making structure; responsibility and responsiveness; resource allocation; local and minority interests; defence needs; contributing or limiting factors; mobility; tolerances

13. Legal

    New laws; administrative restructuring; tax changes; public policy

14. Statutory laws and acts

    Air, water and landscape quality standards; safety standards; national building controls; noise abatement laws

APPENDIX VI

MODEL ENVIRONMENTAL IMPACT ASSESSMENT GUIDELINES

A valuable technique for use in averting environmental degradation is environmental impact assessment, and one example of practical guidelines for environmental impact assessment is set out below.

Man-made works make impact on the environment and there needs to be a workable and economical system which will ensure that those who contemplate potentially harmful actions assess the likely impact upon the environment. In order to protect the environment it is vitally important that this assessment be made prior to any action being taken and that it ranks equally with the technical and economic assessments which always precede development.

An Environmental Impact Statement (EIS) is the best means available for incorporating multi-disciplinary information needed to pass judgement on the various alternatives causing impacts on the environment. It is important to note that the EIS was developed to deal with individual projects and in this regard it is still the best tool available for forging inter-disciplinary links in achieving practical solutions.

The objective of an EIS is to determine:

(i) The characteristics and conditions of the environment prior to the proposed actions.

(ii) The anticipated environmental impact of the proposed actions (and of any alternatives).

(iii) The anticipated impact of the operation of the completed project (and of any alternatives) on the changed environment after the development phase is completed.

An EIS need not be lengthy. It must, however, give clear evidence of data selectively accumulated to allow a calm analysis of the system linkages which in total are the environment itself and from this allow the course of action to be planned in which the most sensitive linkages are given special attention.

An EIS should be constructed taking account of the following basic units, with other material being incorporated if needed:

(i) *Summary*
A concise abstract of the EIS

(ii) *Proposed action*
This section should include information which will enable the decision maker to understand what the proposal is intended to accomplish and to assess its significance in terms of relevant local, regional, provincial and national considerations.

(iii) *Description of the existing environment*
This should detail the existing environment and also draw attention to any unique or rare features, both good and bad, and to the factors which are important to the ecology and amenity of the area. It should be sufficiently

detailed to permit an objective evaluation of the environmental factors, both local and regional, which could be affected by the proposed activities.

The EIS should be accompanied, where appropriate, by quantitative data, maps, photographs, and other relevant exhibits.

Circumstances may exist where, for reasons other than those in the proposal under consideration, the existing environment may be modified in the future and appropriate reference should be made to any relevant known factors or developments.

(iv) *Assessment of impact*

Several methods are available to systematize the assessment of environmental impact, the most favoured being by way of an interaction table in combination with a written statement. In some instances it may be desirable to adopt a method tailored to particular circumstances, but generally the method outlined below will be appropriate. This method presents the assessment in the form of a written statement which:

(a) describes the activities which may cause environmental impacts;

(b) presents the basis on which value judgements have been assigned to these impacts;

(c) discusses the significance of these impacts;

(d) compares the alternative actions which could alter these impacts; and

(e) presents an overall assessment of the environmental impact of the proposal.

The written statement would normally be supported by an interaction table, listing on the horizontal axis all of the activities of the proposal which may cause environmental impact and listing on the vertical axis all of the existing environmental characteristics and conditions which may be affected by proposed actions. Refer to Appendices VII and VIII respectively.

Usually it will be advantageous to assign a carefully considered judgement to each interaction that can occur and to use the resultant listing of interaction points to ensure that a complete evaluation is made.

A sample pro-forma which might be used to construct an interaction table for each alternative plan is presented as Appendix IX.

(v) *Safeguards*

This section should specifically identify the safeguards incorporated in the proposal in order to avoid or minimize adverse environmental effects.

For example, the safeguards may be in the nature of control equipment to reduce the level of atmospheric pollution, liquid effluent treatment plants, erosion control measures or the establishment of a surrounding belt of trees to reduce visual impact or noise.

(vi) *Unavoidable Adverse Effects*

This section should include a review of the unavoidable adverse environmental effects of the proposal, and a reconciliation of the implications of these effects with reasons for proceeding with the proposal.

(vii) *Alternative Courses of Action*

This section should include an analysis of the various alternative means

Appendix VI (*contd.*)

of achieving the project objectives, including competitive benefits and costs (if available), and environmental considerations up to final selection of the preferred proposal. Alternative localities listed in their order of preference should be fully discussed.

The analysis should cover those alternative courses of action, including taking no action, capable of substantially reducing or eliminating adverse effects, even though the alternatives might reduce project objectives or increase project costs.

(viii) *Choice of preferred action*

The environmental, technical and economic investigations associated with the project will highlight a number of diverse but inter-related factors; for example:

- The impact, adverse and beneficial, of the proposed actions on the environment
- Long and short term community benefits
- Cost of the proposed action to the community, including "cost to the environment"

A summary or recommendation which would include the rationale supporting the selected plan should be prepared in this section.

This section should also include an assessment of the extent to which the proposed action permanently pre-empts other desirable uses of the environment.

(ix) *Sources of Information*

Sources of information (reference documents, literature sources, research reports and qualifications of the body or person submitting the document) should be cited in this section.

Important Note

It is almost self-evident that if planners are eventually in the position of being able to use the land capability approach the need for environmental impact statements becomes minimal except for the most major projects or for projects where controversy cannot be settled by appeal to the deterministic properties of the land capability system.

APPENDIX VII

CHECK-LIST OF ACTIVITIES WHICH MAY CAUSE ENVIRONMENTAL
IMPACT

A check-list for deciding the activities of a project which may cause environmental interaction.

1. Siting of facilities

2. Land clearing

3. Burning

4. Blasting

5. Earthworks
    Cutting and filling; excavating; filling; drilling

6. Underground works
    Tunnels; wells; piling; pipelines; cables; conduits; tanks; structures

7. Aboveground works
    Buildings; structures; bridges; processing plant; railways; pipelines; tanks; telephone and power lines; conveyors

8. Waterworks
    Dams; impoundments; weirs, canals; channels, irrigation works; drainage works; sea walls; aquatic structures; piling; submarine pipelines and cables; alteration of river banks and shorelines; alteration of ground water hydrology; diversion of watercourses; control or modification of river flow.

9. Dredging

10. Filling of wetlands

11. Impervious areas
    Roads; pavements; parking areas; airstrips

12. Barriers
    Fences; walls; ditches

13. Signs; hoardings

14. Stockpiling of materials

15. Handling of materials

16. Emissions to atmosphere
    Smoke; grits; dusts; chemicals; gases; acids; hydrocarbons; fumes; odours

Appendix VII (*contd.*)

17. Effluents to waterways

    Solid and liquid wastes; raw or partially treated sewage; treated sewage with high nutrient content; decomposable organic matter; toxic materials such as acids, alkalis, salts of heavy metals; chemicals such as phenols, cyanides; disease producing micro-organisms; radioactive wastes; brines; fats; oils and greases; water treatment wastes; sediments; litter; fertilizers; animal wastes; run-off from agricultural lands including agricultural chemicals; detergents; mine drainage and mineral washings; wastes from watercraft; run-off from roads; cooling water return; irrigation return; leachate from dumps and waste disposal areas

18. Wastes disposed on land

    Solid and liquid industrial wastes; domestic garbage; tailings; slag; spoil; junk; many items listed in 17

19. Generation of traffic

    Pedestrian; road; rail; air; sea; waterway

20. Artificial lighting

21. Communications

22. Noise; vibration

23. Extraction of resources

    Water; minerals; timber; raw materials

24. Renewal of resources

    Replanting of natural areas; re-establishing of land-form; stocking of native fauna; recharge of ground water; recycling of wastes; re-afforestation

25. Development of resources

    Introduction of flora and fauna; improving soil productivity; enhancing marine productivity

26. Protection of resources

    Erosion control; soil conservation; flood control; water conservation; nature conservation

27. Preservation or destruction

    Renewable and non-renewable resources; monuments; features; plants; wildlife

28. Landscaping

    Planting; construction of features; beautification

29. Amenities provided or destroyed

    Facilities for active or passive recreation; access to features or areas

30. Fishing
    Commercial; amateur

31. Hunting
    Commercial; amateur

32. Pleasure boating
    Commercial; amateur

33. Use by Man
    Swimming; boating; camping; hiking; picnicking; sports

34. Accidents
    Operational failures; spills and leaks; explosions; fires

APPENDIX VIII

CHECK-LIST OF CHARACTERISTICS AND CONDITIONS
OF THE ENVIRONMENT

A check-list for deciding the characteristics and conditions of the environment that
may be affected by the activities of the project.

1. *Earth*
   a. Land form
   b. Unique features
   c. Reserves of raw materials
   d. Reserves of minerals
   e. Radiation background
   f. Productive quality of soils
   g. Structural stability of soils
   h. Erosion of soils
   i. Compaction of soils
   j. Dereliction of land
   k. Deposition on land
   l. Flooding
   m. Wetlands
   n. Desertification

2. *Water*
   a. Quality of drinking water
   b. Quantity of drinking water
   c. Quality of surface water
   d. Quantity of surface water
   e. Quality of underground water
   f. Quantity of underground water
   g. Quality of estuarine and ocean
      water
   h. Water temperature
   i. Siltation of waterways
   j. Eutrophication
   k. Salinity

3. *Atmosphere*
   a. Air quality (clarity, particulate
      matter; gases)
   b. Air temperature
   c. Air movements
   d. Climate
   e. Rainfall; snow; ice

4. *Flora*
   a. Trees
   b. Shrubs; herbs
   c. Grass
   d. Crops
   e. Microflora
   f. Aquatic plants including
      phytoplankton
   g. Unique, rare or endangered
      species
   h. Forests
   i. Plant barriers
   j. Plant corridors
   k. Unwanted species
   l. Bushfires

5. *Fauna*
   a. Birds
   b. Land animals including reptiles
   c. Fish and shellfish
   d. Benthic organisms
   e. Insects
   f. Microfauna
   g. Endangered species
   h. Animal barriers
   i. Animal corridors
   j. Unwanted species

6. *Land Use*
   a. Grazing
   b. Agriculture
   c. Residential development
   d. Commercial development
   e. Industrial development
   f. Mining and quarrying

g. Passive recreation
h. Active recreation
i. Resort area
j. Nature conservation
k. Wilderness

7. *Recreation*
   a. Hunting
   b. Fishing
   c. Boating
   d. Swimming
   e. Sporting activities
   f. Camping
   g. Hiking
   h. Picnicking

8. *Cultural*
   a. Scenic views; vistas
   b. Natural bushland
   c. Wilderness areas and qualities
   d. Open space
   e. Wetlands
   f. Landscape design
   g. Unique or rare physical features
   h. Parks and reserves
   i. Playing fields
   j. Monuments
   k. Historical or archaeological
   l. Visual pollution

9. *Amenity*
   a. Personal comfort
   b. Human health
   c. Human safety
   d. Human habitat
   e. Employment
   f. Population density
   g. Life style
   h. Cultural pattern

10. *Ecological Relationships*
    a. Ecosystem structure and function
    b. Rare ecosystems
    c. Nutrient cycling
    d. Disease–insect vectors and introduced hosts
    e. Energy flow and food chains
    f. Synergistic effects

11. *Man-made Facilities*
    a. Buildings and structures
    b. Transportation systems
    c. Utilities distribution systems
    d. Communication systems
    e. Processing plants

APPENDIX IX

ENVIRONMENTAL INTERACTION TABLE

A useful method of considering the possible interactions between the proposed action and the existing environment is the preparation of an "interaction table" or "matrix." A number of different approaches have been devised and references are given below.

Basically the various proposed actions which may cause environmental impact are listed on the horizontal axis of the table and the characteristics and conditions of the environment are listed on the vertical axis. The interactions can be marked or can be given quantitative values according to various procedures. A suggested format is included on the next page.

A number of approaches to the format are possible and it is anticipated that experience in preparation of environmental impact statements will provide a format in agreement with environmental impact policy objectives. It is intended that the format should remain flexible and that the nature and scope of the project, the associated environmental conditions, and the possible adverse effects will dictate the methodology and format used.

It is expected that some government agencies with responsibility for environmental protection will issue guidelines directed specifically towards their own objectives.

Project: Location:
(Indicate alternative being considered)

Characteristics and conditions of the environment	Probability of occurrence of activity	Proposed activities which may cause temporary environmental impact	Proposed activities which may cause permanent environmental impact

APPENDIX X

CLASSIFICATION OF SOME COMMON BIRTH CONTROL METHODS

(A) Without contraceptives					(B) Contraceptives							(c) Surgical		
	Periodic abstinence				Mechanical				Chemical					
						IUD								
Abstinence	Calendar rhythm	Temperature rhythm	Cervical mucus rhythm	Withdrawal	Condom	Loop/coil	Copper 7	Diaphragm	Spermicides	Combination pill	Mini pill	Abortion	Vasectomy	Tubal ligation
(1)	(2)	(3)	(4)	(5)	(6)	(7)	(8)	(9)	(10)	(11)	(12)	(13)	(14)	(15)

Numerous methods of birth control are available. However, there are differing views on their use, safety and effectiveness. The chart above shows some options available.

(A) Without contraceptives

(1) Abstinence

Abstinence, culturally enforced. Preservation of virginity before marriage, late marriage, long lactation without intercourse, celibacy for clergy, isolation of women, taboos associated with menstruation, childbirth and blood ties.

ADVANTAGE

No supplies, preparation or cost. Used intelligently, it can stabilize population by spacing the birth of children. In times of economic hardship a reduced birth rate can avoid additional burdens on families and society.

DISADVANTAGES

Birth rates can sometimes increase due to restricting intercourse to time of fertility. Requires a high degree of personal and community discipline.

(2) Calendar rhythm

Avoiding intercourse during the likely fertile period of about 8 days during a 28-day menstrual cycle, calculated on a formula based on predicting ovulation from an individual's menstrual history.

ADVANTAGES

Requires no artificial, chemical, or other barriers to conception. No cost. No physical side-effects.

DISADVANTAGES

Recorded experience over a number of months is necessary. Requires self-control and self-denial from both partners. Unsuitable for women with irregular menstrual cycles. Can cause psychological stress over possible failure. Inhibition of sexual spontaneity.

(3) Temperature rhythm

Avoiding intercourse during the likely fertile period, calculated by detecting ovulation on the basis of a rise (up to 1°C) in basal body temperature when the egg is released.

ADVANTAGES

Similar to those of "calendar rhythm." Can be more effective when used in combination with "calendar" and "cervical mucus" methods.

DISADVANTAGES

Similar to those of "calendar rhythm." Plus: Cost of thermometer. Illness, emotional tension, lack of sleep and alcohol may influence body temperature. Occasionally, temperature may not rise after ovulation.

(4) Cervical rhythm

Avoiding intercourse during the likely fertile period, calculated by recognizing and interpreting changes in cervical mucus during the menstrual cycle.

ADVANTAGES

Similar to those of "calendar rhythm." Can be more effective when used in combination with "calendar" and "temperature" methods.

DISADVANTAGES

Similar to those of "calendar rhythm." Plus: Messiness. A woman must be sensitive to "dryness" and "wetness" in the external parts of the vagina during the different phases of the menstrual cycle and must be able to differentiate between feelings of "stickiness" and of "lubrication".

(5) Withdrawal

Withdrawal of penis before ejaculation. One of the oldest and most widely used methods.

ADVANTAGES

No supplies, preparation or costs. No apparent disturbance to physical health.

DISADVANTAGES

Escape of semen prior to ejaculation, delayed withdrawal or deposition of semen in the woman's exterior sexual organs can result in pregnancy. Unsuitable for repeat coitus as sperms may survive first intercourse. Possible emotional stresses due to interference with sexual spontaneity. Suitable only for highly motivated couples.

(B) Contraceptives

(6) Condom

A thin, flexible sheath covering the penis to prevent deposition of semen in the vagina. A widely used method.

ADVANTAGES

Offers reliable protection against pregnancy and venereal infection. No physical side-effects.

DISADVANTAGES

Some cost involved. Careless use before and after ejaculation, bursting, tearing and slipping may result in deposition of semen in the vagina. Inhibition of sexual spontaneity. Individual may be allergic to material used.

(7) Loop, coil

Preventing fertilized egg embedding in womb lining by placing a small, flexible device in the womb.

ADVANTAGES

No preparation required before intercourse. Needs to be inserted by a trained person only once for a period of four to five years. Effective almost immediately.

DISADVANTAGES

Should be checked annually by a trained person. Minor problems of heavier bleeding and cramps occurring during three months after insertion. Sometimes spotting or bleeding may occur between menstrual periods, causing inconvenience. State of anaemia in malnourished women may intensify. May cause brief period of pain after insertion, sometimes pelvic inflammation. Cost of device and medical services for fitting.

(8) Copper 7

Preventing fertilized egg embedding in womb lining by placing small, flexible plastic and copper device in the womb.

ADVANTAGES

No preparation required before intercourse. The copper provides an additional contraceptive advantage over earlier interuterine devices. Needs to be inserted by a trained person only once for a period of two years. Effective almost immediately. Small size makes it more suitable for women who have not had children.

DISADVANTAGES

Similar to those of the "loop, coil" IUD. Plus: Unsuitable for women with long intervals between periods.

(9) Diaphragm

A flexible rubber dome-shaped device covering the neck of the womb. It is a mechanical barrier to the entry of sperm into the cervical canal.

ADVANTAGES

Self-fitted. Used every time intercourse occurs, in combination with spermicidal cream or jelly, it can be more effective. No physical side-effects. Lasts 12–18 months if properly cared for.

DISADVANTAGES

Requires initial pelvic examination by trained person to determine correct size. Genital manipulation and possible use of lubricant for insertion. Inconvenience of fitting before intercourse. Must not be removed for eight hours. Inhibition of sexual spontaneity.

(10) Spermicides

Application of chemicals in the form of foams, jellies, creams, suppositories or tablets in the vagina shortly before intercourse to immobilize sperm.

ADVANTAGES

No physical side-effects. Can be more effective when used in combination with other contraceptives such as a diaphragm or condom.

DISADVANTAGES

Requires preparation before intercourse and post-coital care. May cause irritation or inflammatory changes of the vagina mucus membrane. Relatively expensive. Messiness. Excessive lubrication. Inhibition of sexual spontaneity.

(11) Combination pill

A hormone pill of synthetic oestrogen and progestogen, taken daily for 21 days beginning the fifth day after menstruation. It acts to suppress the release of the egg during each menstrual cycle.

ADVANTAGES

Regular pattern of bleeding, closely resembling normal menstruation, is regarded as an attractive feature of the pill. Relatively inexpensive in a developed country, and special type products can be made available at a low cost in developing countries.

DISADVANTAGES

Initial examination and prescription by a trained person needed. Side-effects can include nausea, loss of libido, weight gain, depression, spotting, loss of sex drive, tiredness. Unsuitable for those with severe varicose veins, migraine or liver disease, skin complaints or greasy hair. Changes in blood-clotting system may, in some cases, be risky for those suffering blood-clotting disorders. Vomiting or diarrhoea may stop assimilation of the pill. Cost of pills and medical services.

(12) Mini pill

A pill made of progestogen only, taken continuously daily. It affects mucus at the neck of the womb so that sperm cannot penetrate. It makes the womb lining thinner and therefore unsuitable for a fertilized egg to embed and grow.

ADVANTAGES

Suitable for women who are breastfeeding or who have side-effects from the combined pill.

Appendix X (*contd.*)

DISADVANTAGES

Initial examination and prescription by a trained person needed. Gradual weight gain, depression, loss of libido. Vomiting or diarrhoea may stop assimilation of the pill. Irregular bleeding may sometimes occur, causing inconvenience. Sometimes women continue to ovulate, whereas the combined pill almost invariably prevents ovulation. Cost of pills and medical services.

(C) SURGICAL

(13) Abortion

Termination of pregnancy before the 28th week, that is, the stage before the foetus is regarded as viable and capable of an independent existence. The most widely used method of avoiding unwanted children.

ADVANTAGES

Does not impair sexual sensitivity and prowess. Sometimes used to avoid maternal death or health impairment. Avoidance of the birth of a deficient child.

DISADVANTAGES

Costly. Medical skill is required to ensure success. Can create unpleasant biological and psychological problems.

(14) Vasectomy

Minor surgery to prevent sperm from entering semen, so the egg cannot be fertilized.

ADVANTAGES

Fully effective. Sexual activity continues as normal. In some countries surgery is done at no cost, while substantial rebates are offered in others.

DISADVANTAGES

No guarantee the operation can be reversed (but the sperm may be deposited in a sperm bank before the operation). Occasionally, incision may become infected. Invariably there is pain after the operation. Takes three months to ascertain if operation has been a success. Can have adverse psychological effects. Medical skill required. Cost of post-surgery care.

(15) Tubal ligation

Surgery to fallopian tubes of a female to prevent fertilization taking place.

ADVANTAGES

Similar to "vasectomy" for a male.

DISADVANTAGES

No guarantee that the operation can be reversed. Adverse psychological effects may result. Medical skill required. Cost of post-surgery care.

SELECTED REFERENCES:

Contraception Explained. Clive Wood. WHO, Geneva, 1975.
Population Report. The George Washington University Medical Centre, Washington, D.C.

APPENDIX XI

ENVIRONMENTAL INVESTIGATIONS
(*Format for preliminary survey*)

TABLE 1

Projects listed under subjects

Subject	Project	Institution
Air		
Animals, plants and the land		
Buildings		
Economics		
Engineering		
Fertilizers and manures		
Legal		
Medical		
Mining		
Noise		
Pesticides		
Radioactivity		
Sociological		
Thermal		
Water, estuary and coastal		
Water, inland		

TABLE 2

Projects listed under research institutions

Research institution	Title	Summary	Staff	Finance	Remarks

Index

Action plans 171–6
Administration, environmental 31–6, 58–61
  as a process 53–68
  continuous dialogue framework 153, 160–6
  cyclical nature of 152–4f, 160–6
  inter-related activities 53–4f
  programme administration 65
  surveys of 58–9
    format for 182
Administration, governmental 29–31
Agencies
  co-ordination of approaches 59f
  expertise within (survey format) 184–6
  law administration (survey format) 183
  local 59f
  national 29–30, 33, 108, 110–14
    special 34–5, 108, 110–14ff
  participation in management 157–8
  regional 31, 59f
Ambient standards 74
Appeals and disputes 168
Areas of concern under environmental impact 105–6
  check-list 188–9
Australia
  decentralized government in 30
  environmental bodies 34
  environmental policies and laws 29
  executive body in 25

Background reports 119f, 122, 124, 170
Backward linkage 104f
Biosphere
  constraints imposed by 81–2
  impact of technology on 13ff
Birth control 142–4
  classification of methods 200–4
Biswas, Margaret R. and Asit K. 140

Cabinet system 25, 30, 32
Capital of the land 84
Central planning 99f
Centralized administration 29–30
"City-state" concept 164
Compensation 168–9
Composite land capability maps 121, 123, 127–8
Constitutions 22, 24, 26f
Consultancy methods 47–51
Continuous dialogue
  framework for 153, 160–6
  need for 160
Contraception 142–4
  classification of methods 200–4
Costs, management 84, 86
Councils of Ministers 32–3
Crises, forestalling 176
Cyclic ecological changes 84–6

Data gathering 48–50, 170
Decentralized administration 30–1